DUTY BOUND

DUTY BOUND

Responsibility and American Public Life

MARK BLITZ

ROWMAN & LITTLEFIELD PUBLISHERS, INC.
Lanham • Boulder • New York • Toronto • Oxford

ROWMAN & LITTLEFIELD PUBLISHERS, INC.

Published in the United States of America
by Rowman & Littlefield Publishers, Inc.
A wholly owned subsidary of
The Rowman & Littlefield Publishing Group, Inc.
4501 Forbes Boulevard, Suite 200, Lanham, Maryland 20706
www.rowmanlittlefield.com

PO Box 317
Oxford
OX2 9RU, UK

British Library Cataloging in Publication Information Available

Library of Congress Cataloging-in-Publication Data

Blitz, Mark.
    Duty bound : responsibility and American public life / Mark Blitz.
    p. cm.
    Includes index.
    ISBN 0-7425-3301-8 (cloth : alk. paper) — ISBN 0-7425-3302-6
(pbk. : alk. paper)
    1. Political ethics. 2. Responsibility—Political aspects. 3. Political ethics—
United States. 4. Responsibility—Political aspects—United States.
5. Responsibility—Philosophy.   I. Title.
JA75.7.B59 2005
323.6'5'0973—dc22

                                                          2004019984

Printed in the United States of America

∞™ The paper used in this publication meets the minimum requirements of
American National Standard for Information Sciences—Permanence of Paper
for Printed Library Materials, ANSI/NISO Z39.48-1992.

ACC Library Services
Austin, Texas

To Ellen, Daniel, and Adam

CONTENTS

ACKNOWLEDGMENTS

I would like to thank the following for permission to adapt earlier publications and lectures: Rowman & Littlefield Publishers, Inc., the University of Nebraska Press, the American Enterprise Institute for Public Policy Research, the Hudson Institute, the Ethics and Public Policy Center, and the Helen Dwight Reid Educational Foundation's *Perspectives on Political Science.*

Colleagues at Claremont McKenna College and associates at various Liberty Fund colloquia improved this book, as did my reviewers and editors at Rowman & Littlefield. The John M. Olin Foundation, Lynde and Harry Bradley Foundation, and Earhart Foundation have provided funding that has supported my work. I am pleased to acknowledge their generosity.

INTRODUCTION

Every book should have a theme, and mine is that the aim of a healthy liberal democracy is to produce characteristic types of human beings—namely, responsible ones. Responsibility is the defining element of liberal character, and liberal democracy works best when responsibility flourishes.

Responsibility presents itself as a candidate to be the central goal and mechanism of successful liberal democracies because of its correlation with liberty: We constantly say that our rights and freedoms should be used responsibly. Responsibility, as the twin of liberty, is its proper limit and guide.[1]

Responsibility recommends itself as liberal democracy's guide and goal also because it is a new virtue, or at least one that is newly named. It is mentioned first around the time of the American founding, notably in *The Federalist Papers*. It therefore shares the novelty of American liberal democracy itself.

SCOPE

My initial task is to specify what responsibility is and to show its significance for liberal democracy. I do this in my first chapter; there I define and discuss responsibility in conjunction with the other characteristic virtues of modern democracies: tolerance, industry, and niceness (or kindness). My first departure from usual discussions of responsibility is to emphasize its link to accomplishing things effectively and successfully rather than to punishment and guilt. My second is to

1

show how responsibility is the primary virtue that answers a question that lies at the heart of liberal democracy: How can a way of life that emphasizes self-interest summon attention to common efforts?

I then explore responsibility in politics, where its importance as both outcome and mechanism of successful institutions is most visible. Liberal democracy seeks to liberate responsibility and then uses it within government and among citizens. I first employ it to explain how bureaucracies and the separation of powers work. I then make responsibility my guide for understanding the purpose and direction of foreign policy, which should be neither "idealistic" nor "realistic" but—responsible. I do not intend to ignore the importance of other concepts that help explain free government, but I link them to responsibility, my organizing thread.

I turn next to how responsibility functions in the professions. "Professional responsibility" is an important object of training, study, and informed opinion. I examine critically the link between responsible character and the conditions for success in law, journalism, education, and philanthropy. I also discuss the connections among liberty, responsibility, and the ends the professions serve. One of my general goals is to clarify the nature of goods as we experience them today and to show that ours is but one way to experience them generally.

This more theoretical turn leads to my book's final part, where I explore responsibility's future and limits. I first discuss responsibility and biotechnology, for biotechnology raises serious practical and theoretical issues about liberalism and human purpose. By analyzing its promise and threat I hope to combine my political, professional, and theoretical themes. I conclude by discussing John Locke, thereby placing liberalism and responsibility in a philosophical context and returning to issues on which I touched at the start.

METHOD

My mention of theory and philosophy should call to mind questions about the book's scope and method. I do not discuss responsibility in every aspect of American life. Those looking to read about responsibility in the arts or religion will look in vain, as will those wishing to hear about the family or business generally. My book is about public life and the public face or direction of private life, not about private life simply. Because I emphasize the serious (or even ponderous) notion of responsibility, moreover, I cannot dwell upon what is playful and light. That said, toleration is a central modern virtue; our professions and philanthropy are businesses or stem from them; education is at home with "culture," and, therefore, also with playful leisure and fine arts; and biotechnology brings to the surface deep questions about the family and its roots. So I have something to say even about what I do not discuss systematically.

My "method" deserves a word as well. Explicit methodology is a construct of natural science and its imitation in social science. We look at things through defined procedures that are alien to the way we usually deal with them and to the problems with which practice presents us. Matters are broken down or analyzed into parts—often equivalent, countable parts—and built up again. A visible success of this direction is political polling. A visible failure is explaining prudent statesmanship and the qualities of good legislation.

Rather than employing an explicit methodology, I use various methods that attempt to track the practical existence of the things I study and the issues they raise. I sometimes begin from ordinary opinions and seek the root or defining meanings that underlie them. At other times I begin from current issues, exhortations, and concerns, seeking the ground that guides and explains them. In still other instances I seek to unravel the function of an institution as it works responsibly within liberal democracy as a whole.

The purpose of these excursions is to find the general forms that organize the institutions of liberal democracy in advance and to uncover the way institutions actually operate to energize them. We confront and deal with the specific facts and activities of, say, law, politics, and the media within these shapes, which give them their meaning and importance. They set the directions within which technical, instrumental, or merely moralistic thinking occurs.[2] Responsibility is an especially important element of these forms, because responsible action is both goal and practice, both end and active form, in liberal democracy generally. In discussing institutions I therefore rely more on articulating opinions and practices that we take for granted than on a wealth of factual detail. Forms make facts relevant in the first place. Nonetheless, I obviously have in mind, and refer to, many facts and empirical generalizations. In doing so, I rely especially on the example of the United States.

What gives our institutions direction and worth is always something of an aspiration. I also emphasize responsibility to indicate that what defines our practices is not automatic or self-perpetuating but requires effort and risk. I therefore will point out institutions' characteristic failures and challenges. Not only do our practices fail to realize fully all that shapes them, but liberal democracy itself falls short. Even the most just legal profession will never embody justice simply.

The procedure I am discussing guided from the outset all sections of the book, each of which, whether newly appearing, revised, or largely taken from previous efforts, was from the beginning written with the whole in mind.

PHILOSOPHY

The judgment that understanding requires an explicit methodology is rooted in philosophy. Descartes's *Discourse on Method* comes readily to mind. Although I present my procedure merely as following liberal opinion, politics, and institutions to their organizing form and then back again, one might reasonably doubt the honesty of this seeming naïveté. After all, my argument relies on notions of form, cause, desire, spirit, generality, and the like that self-consciously differ from analytic or experimental methodology. I address liberal democracy, its freedom, institutions, and virtues, in a certain way, apparently conceived in advance. When I pursue links between goals, character, and institutions, for example, I have in mind the classical philosophers' discussions of arts and regimes. (Some of my chapters are, as it were, studies in Platonic political science.) When I employ a sense of the moral ontology of liberalism—the link among its organizing concepts, practices, and limits—this sense is not isolated but points to other moral ontologies.

I raise these issues—and in that way defend my method against "methodology"—in the book's concluding chapters and in various places along the way. Suffice it to say here that the richer whole that responsibility and liberal institutions exemplify can itself be approached along the commonsensical path I take in discussing liberalism.

NOTES

1. Calling for responsibility has been a special hallmark of recent presidential administrations. Consider, for example, President George W. Bush's 2004 State of the Union address. It also is a feature of the rhetoric of Vaclav Havel as he discusses how to confront Czech communism, as well as of Winston Churchill's political understanding. See "The Power of the Powerless" (especially sections XIV, XV, XVIII, and XIX) in Vaclav Havel, *Open Letters*, sel. and ed. Paul Wilson (New York: Vintage Books, 1992); Winston S. Churchill, *The Gathering Storm* (New York: Houghton Mifflin, 1948), passim; and various speeches (for example, one delivered at Harvard University on September 6, 1943) gathered in Kay Halle, ed. *Winston Churchill on America and Britain* (New York: Walker, 1970).

2. One of my goals is to differentiate both practical and theoretical understanding of liberal democracy and morality from such ultimately secondary standpoints.

1

RESPONSIBILITY AND MODERN VIRTUE

Responsibility is one of several virtues we consider good today that the ancient thinkers who first discussed character did not analyze or praise. This fact should make us wonder. If Aristotle, with his brilliance and comprehensiveness, did not consider something to be a virtue, why should we?[1] To see responsibility's distinctive place, novelty, and link to freedom, it is helpful to consider it in conjunction with the other "modern" virtues. In turn, this allows us to discover the leading characteristics of such virtues generally and some common elements of modernity overall. I begin with the quality of "niceness," or being nice (and its relatives kindness and compassion), because it is so far from ancient or warrior virtues that it helps to bring out the novelty of modernity generally. I then turn to two other characteristic modern virtues—tolerance and industry—and conclude with responsibility.

BEING NICE

Let us begin with "niceness."[2] When we tell someone, normally a child, to be "nice," it is usually after he has done something rotten, such as destroying his sister's elaborate dollhouse, often cackling with pleasure at his handiwork. Not to be nice is to pay little or no attention to others' happiness and desires while pursuing one's own interest, however fleeting and casual. In the more extreme case, it is to enjoy causing someone else's unhappiness; in the still more extreme sense, it is to be a habitually malicious bully. For tamed adults, the

7

equivalent is to be nice by not being sarcastic, ironic, or, as we sometimes now say, "hurtful." To be nice means not to be "bad" in the
sense of not being selfish, "mean," or spiteful, or to be good in the
sense of being helpful or "kind."

Occasionally, we tell a child to be nice after she has done something intrusively annoying, such as incessantly whining or complaining. "Please be nice, and leave me alone for a minute." Here, to be
nice means not to be thoughtless and "inconsiderate." Someone nice
does not merely pay attention to others' interests but, primarily, pays
attention to them, or to their feelings, as he pursues his own interests.
Sometimes, indeed, we prospectively enjoin, or beg, children to be
nice, when their grandparents are about to visit, for example, and we
fear they will be their usual rude, distant, and selfish selves. Here, to
be nice is to go a bit out of one's way in order to be considerate. It
means to attend, at least a little, directly to others. So, to be nice is to
be helpful or considerate or, more often, not to be inconsiderate or
mean. Nice people are well mannered and well behaved ("civil," not
rude), though not, as such, outstandingly courteous.

The case in which a child willfully spills his milk nicely com-
bines the nuances of this meaning: the child is not "nice," because he
intentionally makes someone unhappy by inconsiderately forcing her
to attend to him. (This is early training for the characteristic adoles-
cent nastiness of purposely ruining one's parents' pleasant evening by
forcing them to bail one out of trouble.) Perhaps the best example is
the evil mother, beloved of stage and screen, who chooses the moment of her spinster daughter's first important date to think that she
has become, or to pretend to think that she has become, deathly ill.
The nice person does not "impose" herself on others; the mean person inconsiderately imposes herself on others; the truly mean, or malicious, person imposes herself on others primarily in order to make
them miserable.

We approach the second major sense of being "nice" by considering what we mean when we speak of a "nice" teacher or boss. The
nice employer or professor is undemanding. He forgives mistakes easily. He listens to excuses and allows them to sway him. He accepts late
papers and lets people leave early on Friday afternoons. He is not a
rigid stickler for bureaucratic rules or for the set forms by which we

are supposed to carry out tasks. To be nice in this sense is a variant of being merciful: to be nice is to be flexible, to be willing to bend, to not always force students or employees to live up to standards, principles, or practices they may find alien, difficult, or unfair. The nice professor also is approachable, even gentle, because one senses he is willing to listen and to compromise, or even to give in: he is soft, not hard; "reasonable," not prickly; pliant, not "tough." He does not always demand his own way.

In addition to flexibility and consideration, niceness also refers to a third characteristic, general friendliness, or, more precisely, general pleasantness. As we suggested, the nice man is as much (or more) someone who is not harmful or inconsiderate as he is one who is actively helpful or evenhanded. "Pleasantness" is the positive portrayal or display of this withdrawal or restraint. Similarly, a "nice" time or event is a generally pleasant or merely innocuous time, not an outstanding, noteworthy, or demanding time. "That was a nice symphony [game, meal, book, stretch of weather]." In this sense, "nice" is broadly synonymous with good, with emphasis on the pleasant and undemanding but without always being so limited. In short, then, to be nice is to be flexible, helpful, pleasant, and considerate, or at least not rigid, harmful, nasty, or inconsiderate. The chief characteristic of being nice is not always to demand one's own way, whether that way is proper behavior according to a standard or following one's malicious or even reasonable desires. The nice person is considerate of others' wishes, possessions, and feelings.

About what is one flexible and considerate? Anything, at least potentially. There is no set of goods toward which niceness is the proper disposition, because one can be nice or nasty, helpful or harmful, considerate or inconsiderate, flexible or rigid, about nearly anything or anyone. Nonetheless, one usually is nice or nasty toward other people, and when one destroys their things the nastiness is toward the owner, not toward the things themselves.

A further sense is visible when we say that someone makes a nice distinction, point, or argument. Here nice means small or narrow, usually in the favorable sense of subtle, precise, graceful, and refined, or at least careful and not trivially obvious. "Nice" manners are "good" in the sense of careful, though not quite superb. Nice, as in the exclamation "Nice!" after an especially good move in sports, also means apt, precise, or appropriate. Nice as good, therefore, does not only mean pleasant but also refers to a not too taxing, if not quite egalitarian, sense of beauty or refinement.

In summary, someone nice does not always demand his own way and considers, and often gives in to, others' interests and feelings. He is pleasant and not a bully. One can be nice about anything or toward anyone, and we can call almost anything nice.

We can explain how "nice" and good are synonymous, and even how nice as appropriate and refined is not merely homonymous with nice as pleasant, by reflecting on the equality and universality characteristic of modern liberal democracies. Niceness is a virtue more akin to the moderation and justice of which nearly all men and women seem capable than to the courage or, especially, pride of a few. Unlike classic moderation, however, it is not restricted to pleasures but covers nearly anything. Niceness is at one with the equal respect that modern political thought tells us we all deserve. It presupposes liberalism's lack of hierarchy among goods and its view that goods are only what happen to meet our desires and become our interests. Niceness is connected to "kindness," where to be kind is to be mild and gentle—that is, to treat our human "kind" as what we share equally and easily, rather than as characteristics that differentiate us and need tutoring and education. In fact, niceness as a virtue can oppose the rigorous standards we otherwise claim to admire, for demanding that others live up to standards is to seem inflexible, unfeeling, arbitrary, or selfish. One is imposing one's own way, even if it is a way we claim to be generally correct.

We moderns do not believe that being nice is an unmixed blessing. One can be "too nice," and there always exists the lingering sense that whoever is nice isn't tough enough—that to be nice is always to be too nice. Nice guys finish last, as the saying goes. This does not mean only that they obtain less of what interests them than do rigid, inflexible, bullies but that they obtain less of what they deserve.[3] In practice this means that one deserves whatever one is strong and lucky enough to obtain in a regime where all goods are equal opportunities—that is, where everyone by nature has an equal right to everything. Nice guys obtain less than they "deserve" because they are too weak to take as much as their talents normally would bring them, given (or making) some luck. One wants a business partner or commanding officer to be nice to oneself but not to the enemy. One even recognizes that common success might demand a boss who is tough to subordinates. So, although being nice is a seemingly unprecedented general virtue that applies to almost all goods, its sway has not destroyed all understanding of its limits.

The virtue of being nice (and of kindness) is similar but not identical to the modern virtue of compassion. The likeness is in the mildness and gentleness, and in the breadth of men (and animals) toward whom one feels it. But compassion normally is felt for those who suffer; it is empathy with the miserable and sad, not philosophic understanding of all things, large and small. Nice men, on the other hand, let others have their way not so much because they feel their pain as because they think it unfair to demand too much. Indeed, while compassion is a feeling for one's kind, niceness is not truly a feeling but a disposition. To be nice sometimes requires a bit of thought and discrimination about the appropriate and deserving, while to be compassionate is simply to feel. One feels compassion, but one *is* nice. Being nice is a disposition that may be supported by compassion, empathy, or gentleness (rather than by anger and indignation), but, especially as a synonym for fairness, it trains these passions rather than simply following them. Finally, although "nice" is synonymous with much that is good, "compassionate" is not: it does not duplicate the senses of nice as pleasant, refined, or fitting.[4]

TOLERANCE

Tolerance is a second virtue for which there is no exact classical equivalent. It apparently is a species of moderation, but moderation is about pleasure, not belief; it defines proper behavior toward those of other faiths but does not as such replace pious reverence for the god in whom one believes and for his commands. As is true of niceness, tolerance is a disposition, not a feeling: it is a habit that must be learned, and it takes training, though not terribly much, to exercise it intelligently. As also is true of niceness, it may be supported by such passions or moods as calm, gentleness, and mildness rather than by indignation or tension. In fact, it is a trained control of spirited self-assertion or indignation, training that is then supported by milder passions.

To be tolerant is to permit others to do things their own way. One does not interfere with them, although one need not help them. Nowadays, toleration covers more than religion. Indeed, that we tolerate primarily those of different faiths is almost forgotten; we are more often asked to be, or fail to be, tolerant of spendthriftiness, cowardice, stupidity, or pleasure seeking. Normally we are enjoined to tolerate ingrained customs and habits, but not always; we also can be asked to tolerate unexpected delays or an unexpected display of temper.

To be tolerant is not necessarily to approve what one tolerates. In fact, the tolerant man traditionally permits or allows what he does not approve. These days, however, people called tolerant or very tolerant seem not to disapprove at all. At least, they keep their disapproval so much to themselves that they seem not to disapprove. Indeed, the difference between tolerating and approving is (in some quarters) fast disappearing; tolerant men often are asked to support and not merely to allow.

Tolerance began as what some believed to be the proper individual and legislative disposition toward believers in religions other than the reigning Protestantism.[5] Its effect, in fact, is to neutralize (or Protestantize) all religions by tempering their most excessive political claims. When we expand the use of "tolerance" beyond religion per se, it is quite close to niceness. One shade of difference is that while someone is nice to those over whom he would otherwise ride roughshod, the physically weak, those to whom he is indifferent, and those who fail to live up to his standards, we normally are asked to be tolerant of others' faults, difficulties, and weakness, not of people we would thoughtlessly ignore. "He doesn't tolerate mistakes"—this retains the sense that we tolerate action and behavior we disapprove or are expected to disapprove. A second shade of difference is that while selfish is one apt opposite of nice, it is not a terribly apt opposite of tolerant. Rigid or tough, which also can oppose being nice, are more apt. To tolerate foibles is to accept what one disapproves; to be nice to the weak is not to force them to obey one. To be tolerant is not so much about unselfishly failing to impose one's status, will, and desires;

rather, it is not to impose completely one's way of life and principles or codes.

A third and manifest difference is that while nice is a synonym for good, the tolerable is that which barely passes muster. This is connected to the fact that while we tolerate what we disapprove, niceness qua niceness treats others as equal to us. In this sense, niceness is a broader virtue than tolerance, because it is a form of seemingly just treatment of others and affirmatively covers good things, while tolerance covers others' foolishness or beliefs—that is, something about them, but not them. Though anything, from food to philosophy textbooks, can be called tolerable, being simply tolerable is not very good. This is not to deny, as we said, that tolerant and nice are sometimes close to synonymous, that to call someone tolerant often is to single out an aspect of his niceness. This resemblance is caused by niceness's greater breadth as a virtue that tries to treat someone fairly in general, when "fairly" means equally in all respects. In another sense, however, this breadth itself belongs to modernity's decline from legal respect for others' equality in rights to a bland equality in which all goods and people are equal.

From this point of view, indeed, being nice is a decline from tolerance, which speaks less to insipid equality. Tolerance retains a sense that it is about important things—about grudgingly permitting others' freedom but not dominance, in religion, customs, and ways of life. To the extent that tolerance is not simply one version of being nice, as it largely is today, it is nobler, because it requires restraint that is less visibly good than the nice man's overcoming selfishness, and it is certainly about something higher. Of course, to the degree that being nice truly echoes the original modern equality in rights, we should think even of tolerance as merely part of this broader sense of modern justice. Tolerance too, for all the height of its primary object, is, as a kind of motion, neither the awful shuddering within which one's own self-enclosed dignity and pride come to light and are protected nor worshipful, uplifting love. As is true of being nice, it is a kind of flexibility, a lack of angry, spirited, defense or protection. At its extreme, to permit all is cowardly flaccidity. Tolerance is a kind of steady, indifferent, movement, the effect of which is to equalize in blandness the religious heights that were its original object and the compelling secular concerns that are its contemporary field.

INDUSTRIOUSNESS

We also think hard work or industriousness is a virtue. It is better to work hard than to be lazy. This is not to say that playful ease, grace, good manners, and charm are not virtues also or that they simply are opposed to hard work. One can be both industrious and graceful, even charming. Yet there is a seriousness or earnestness in hard work, especially in the display and appearance of industry, that rests uneasily with playful grace and charm. Even the graceful masking of earnestness is no longer seen to be unambiguously good, because we often believe we ought to appear to work hard.

Although we sometimes say that people work too hard, this usually means that they are working too hard for their own good—that is, that they need a rest so they will be able to work more effectively in the future. Working too hard is chiefly a mistake only in terms of work itself, with the notion that one should nonetheless sometimes stop to smell the roses, an occasional reminder that playful grace and moderate enjoyment of pleasure are virtues too.

What is industriousness? To be industrious is to work hard, sometimes with great energy but as often with mere dogged determination. To be industrious is to persevere in one's assignment. The responsible man, whom we will discuss shortly, also may persevere, but he is better understood as one who sees to it that the job is done correctly, that the intention behind the effort actually is satisfied, not merely that the project is pursued diligently. The responsible man, therefore, has in view the purpose of the task and its place in the larger whole; indeed, sometimes he exercises his responsibility as a commander or supervisor with a bit of distance, seeing to it that things are going right without himself moving the machine.[6] The industrious man works diligently at his task and, as such, need not have in mind the larger task at all: there is something dull-witted and dronelike about mere industry.[7]

The industrious man perseveres in his assignments—but what are they? One can be industrious about anything under the sun. As is true of the other modern virtues, there is no special good toward which it is the proper disposition, as moderation is to pleasure, courage to fear, liberality to wealth, or pride to honor. We more often are said to be industrious about things or activities than about people, but we also are enjoined to be industrious about, to "work hard at," our "relationships." Moreover, we can be industrious about plotting murders and stealing funds as well as about catching criminals and investing savings. We might not be enjoined to be hardworking criminals, but diligence as such, its quality and range qua diligence, does not seem to be affected by its purpose—at least, we do not talk as if it is.

Industriousness is diligent perseverance in carrying out or working through assignments. As a form of motion (and all virtues are some kind or combination of attraction, repulsion, inclusion, and separation), it is a gathering of oneself, but not for the moderate redirection of longing and being uplifted that spends itself pleasantly in enjoyment or exhaustion. Rather, it is a gathering of oneself simply for subsequent motion to and from one thing after another, with the ending or cessation not being fulfilling or exhausting but, instead, of such quality that the movement can be picked up, as it were, precisely where it has been left off. The job is not done in the sense of being completely realized as much as in the sense of being over: the last file has been filed, but when another file is found it too will be filed, with no loss or gain to a whole with defined parts.

Naturally, we sometimes talk of industriousness in ways that connect it to working on something beautiful or refined, a work of fine or manual art. But the model of industriousness is more the movement of one thing after another, linking links in a chain that stops from time to time but is not going anywhere. In this sense, the fact that we can be called industrious about anything—beautiful productions and magnificent actions in battle as well as work in an office—means that all goods are seen in flat similarity when we see them as subjects of industrious activity. Hard work is the activity of producing and accumulating the goods that satisfy the flat desires of modern man. It is no accident that industriousness is the obvious virtue that defines modern (bourgeois) man, for whom desire can be for anything with equal legitimacy and for whom satisfaction is a momentary resting, not a grand embracing. The industrious pursuit of satisfaction, the laborious accumulation and securing of the resources (the goods) that allow this satisfaction, and the (near) identity of moving through one's tasks, accumulating goods (interests and property), and satisfying desires make industriousness equally a means and an end in modern life.

RESPONSIBILITY

A fourth distinctively modern virtue, and the theme of this book, is responsibility. As we noted, responsibility displays its modernity by being named first around the time *The Federalist Papers* were written. Politicians of the Left and Right now discuss it incessantly. What is responsibility? When we call people responsible we mean, first, to hold them to account. From childhood on we are asked who is responsible for making a mess or leaving a chore undone. Later, we seek to find the person responsible for a patient's untimely death or a poorly constructed house. That is, we look for the one at fault, someone to blame. In this sense, to feel responsibility means to feel "guilt," to feel worthy of punishment and blame. But when are we deservedly accountable, not just blamed arbitrarily? We are accountable when we cause the mistake or wrong rather than, say, because we have been ritually selected as a sacrifice to redress it or because an ancestor's misdeed makes us blameworthy. Our second meaning of responsibility is to be something's cause, the reason it happened.[8] Most academic discussion of responsibility concentrates on this notion, or on the link between blame and causality, because its focus is on the conundrum of "free will" and determinism.[9]

Accountability and guilt make us think of intention and sin, qualities and vices of the head and the heart. Responsibility's third main meaning, however, indicates something different, for to call a man responsible suggests that he concerns himself with results and sees to it that the results are correct. A responsible physician or builder sees his work, his responsibility, through to its end and takes care that it is done well. He is reliable and dependable. Good intentions are insufficient; indeed, we often will look away from motives if the job always is done right. (Though responsibility in the sense of accountability often is negative—we look for the "responsible" official when we wish to complain, and we hold people to account when they make mistakes—we mean to praise someone when we call him responsible in the sense of reliable.)

We can gather these meanings together and say that to be responsible is to be accountable for results, for outcomes, because one has effected (or failed to effect) them. To whom are we accountable? Most obviously and immediately, we account to those for whom we are working, to those who have given us our responsibilities. In this sense we often ask those responsible to be "responsive," by which we mean that they should dance more quickly to our tunes.[10] From a somewhat more reflective point of view, however, to encourage people to be responsible is to encourage them to be accountable to themselves for their own effectiveness: we encourage them to bring about and practice the traits and skills that enable them to be successful, today and in the future. Responsibility is the disposition not just to be effective but to secure one's effectiveness. When we call politicians who worry about budget deficits responsible or ask people to use alcohol responsibly, we have in mind the prudence and care that look to the future.

Responsibility, however, means more than doing one's own job effectively. We also think of responsible men as ones who take charge of tasks that seem to belong to nobody in particular, situations where no one is obviously accountable and circumstances that no one seems to have caused. To be responsible is to take charge after a flood when no one else knows what to do, or to work to make a successful request to a local government for more neighborhood police when no one else volunteers. Responsibility in this sense means taking on common tasks and seeing them through: a responsible man's actions go beyond doing and being accountable for his job, because he makes things his job. The responsible man holds himself accountable when he need not, although soon enough everyone expects him always to act responsibly. Responsible men and women often are the ones we urge to enter politics, because they bring results that are commonly good, good for others as well as themselves.

This final meaning of responsibility might lead us to believe that it is an ancient virtue, newly named. Although it clearly is connected to nobility, however, it is at root modern. For, responsibility fits with liberal self-interest rather than being contrary to it, as it might seem.

It is not alien to self-interest as is altruism, or preliberal (as is the classic virtue of pride), or religious duty, although it is related to them. It is their analogue, transformed to be consistent with the accumulating nature of the modern liberal self and the always voluntary nature of his attachments. In this sense, it is part of the same general understanding of goodness, satisfaction, and their breadth that we observed with the other modern virtues.

We can see this better if we consider more carefully what we are seeking when we attempt to be responsible for ourselves. If I habitually spend lavishly, waste my time, or do not study, I am properly accused of being irresponsible. This means that what I am doing now will make it hard to satisfy my desires effectively in the future. Being responsible about oneself is a disposition of character whereby I treat myself as a possibility for continued accumulation. Self-interested behavior, that is to say, is not ultimately for the sake of any particular narrow attachment but for the sake of self-perpetuation. Because this is the goal, one begins to develop habits of steadiness, reliability, foresight, and expansiveness, and a self defined by these characteristics; these habits, indeed, are the conditions for successfully exercising economic and other rights. The link between rights and responsibilities is not that others' rights cause a defined reciprocal responsibility. It is unclear, for example, what affirmative responsibility your right to free speech imposes on me; I am at best accountable if I interfere with you illegally. This is a negative and weak form of responsibility. The truer link between rights and responsibility comes from responsibility's being the disposition to exercise one's own rights effectively when others hold equal rights; one therefore becomes reliable enough to give oneself and others their due. Responsibility is the disposition to take charge and effectively execute the tasks one takes on freely.

This attachment to self-perpetuation and the disposition to take charge can, on reflection, lead some of us quite naturally to take an ever-greater long-term and common point of view. For, there is good reason to think that one's own cool, measured, calculated, ongoing attachment and accumulation will be more successfully perpetuated in the broad field of serving or shaping others than in the small domains of petty interest. Moreover, one grasps and experiences one's freedoms and oneself more and more fully as one effectuates them—exercises responsibility—in wider and wider realms. In fact: given full competition, a long-range, expansive, and (one might say) imperialist perspective is needed even to stand still.

So, as some of us piece by piece make the growth and effectiveness of this responsible self our actual goal, we do increasingly responsible things, such as serving long-range common institutions, even though the equal and interchangeable nature of participation in these institutions at first makes it unclear why anyone should give time to them. There is a continuum, resting on responsibility for oneself, that leads from responsibility for what most exclusively belongs to and rests on oneself (say, one's family) to responsibility as doing one's job well, to responsibility experienced as making one's own the common tasks, such as political service, that need to be done but belong to no one. Responsibility activates itself as the attempt to be effective in public as well as private tasks, to look at the effects of one's actions in ever-wider areas, and to consider all this in a manner that attends to the conditions needed for the successful pursuit of one's own interests.

In saying this, I have more in mind than what we call "enlightened self-interest." Rather, what happens on one's progression is that we understand the self and our disposition to be responsible to it in broader ways. It becomes a matter of character, not only of calculation—that is, responsibility becomes a virtue. I also am not suggesting that everyone will be equally responsible but rather that the steadier my responsibility, the firmer my self-interest, and the fuller my exercise of rights, the wider will be my grasp of the true requirements of common tasks. Moreover, although the most responsible men take charge of political tasks that belong to no one (or no class) in particular, their disposition leads them especially to attend effectively to what is singular or unavoidable within those tasks—national security, say, or aid to others that must come from one's own country or not at all.

The fully responsible man clearly opens in the direction of pride and nobility and needs to exercise more than ordinary fairness. Although responsibility points or belongs to a natural virtue, it more obviously indicates the transformation of classic virtue in the modern world. Just as the public "interest" is similar but not identical to the common "good," responsibility belongs to a different way of seeking, finding, and holding. Responsible men's actions stem less from an attraction to honorable independence and beautiful completion than from the aspiration to accumulate for and satisfy themselves. They typically act in situations where the common benefit is also a more or less identical individual benefit to them, rather than acting because ruling a common enterprise is their own characteristic natural field and place.[11]

THE CHARACTERISTICS OF MODERN VIRTUE

We may now gather together and summarize the salient points of our descriptions, in order to touch upon what is distinctive in responsibility and the other modern virtues. First, modern virtues deal with all goods without discrimination. There is nothing about which one cannot in some regard be tolerant, responsible, industrious, or nice. Second, modern virtues allow equal access, in the sense that very little equipment is needed for them (the rich can be as virtuous as the poor) and in the sense that one man's exercising the virtue does not detract from another's exercising it. The exception here is the fullest meaning of responsibility.

Third, each of these virtues displays lack of driving motion, or lack of uplifting passion, especially when compared to the classic virtue that it resembles or supplants. The nice or compassionate man is neither a spirited guardian of justice nor a cauldron of desire who seeks to moderate his passions lest they overwhelm him. The industrious man is neither the ambitious man who directs and redirects a driving wish for honor nor the steely protector of home and fatherland. His industry (and energy) lack direction as such. Tolerance is less the careful containment of passionate love of what is honorable, right, and true than the easy exercise of mild forbearance. Further, the responsible man does not hunger for pride of place or for the beautiful completion of a noble enterprise so much as he does what he must. In general, modern virtue does not control yearning or fierceness but, rather, smoothes out and restrains what is rough in order to keep things moving along.

Fourth, just as modern virtues require little equipment, they do not need much prudence or practical reason. To be nice or tolerant requires some judgment and thoughtful balance but not a great deal, nor do they require much experience. This is why these virtues sometimes seem to be only the visible expression of mild native dispositions rather than the habitual and prudential direction of passions. Industriousness as such requires little prudence, although useful industry needs the thought of the artisan or owner who sets things in motion. Responsibility, the virtue most obviously echoing ruling and nobility, also is the virtue most closely tied to practical intelligence. This is clearest when we think of responsible men as taking on jobs that are no one's in particular. But responsibility also means, more broadly if less significantly, getting one's own job done. It therefore often requires merely that one recognizes one's job and has or acquires the tools to do it. The degree of required practical wisdom or deliberative judgment and skill may be minimal, or it may be great; this depends upon the job and its author.[12]

The fifth distinctive characteristic of the modern virtues is that none of them, again with the partial exception of responsibility, is so desirable in itself that it seems to be a necessary part of human excellence. Indeed, it is strange to think of them as excellent at all. Taken together, niceness (compassion), tolerance, industriousness, and responsibility (as accountability) lack splendor. That "virtue" should describe the well-formed character that is the goal of education would hardly be obvious were the modern virtues all that there is to virtue. This deficiency is not caused simply by my separating moral from intellectual virtue here, for the classical splendor of the statesman or gentleman was not fully tarnished by this separation. Nor is it altogether caused by the fact that we have displaced political and spirited virtues from their classical home, for the modern virtues (as a group) also lack the luster of the "Christian" virtues of service, faith, and humility.

The fact that modern virtues do not present themselves as required for human excellence is not so surprising once we recall their other features—the equality of the goods with which they deal and people who can hold them, the flatness of motion that impels them and that they direct and redirect, and the absence of a necessarily accompanying practical wisdom and deliberation. Modern virtues are as much means as ends for individuals and for the institutions that serve them. They belong to and help secure and perpetuate the restless motion, the accumulation of goods (interests) with which we continue this motion, and the occasional resting (or "satisfaction") that renews energy for the uneasy flight that is the heart of modern happiness. No modern virtue is above being used poorly, because the goods correlated to them are so variable, all display their Machiavellian origin. Nonetheless, because they express equally held rights, they can be pursued fully within boundaries that limit them properly. Even the breadth of effective responsibility works within a community of natural equals. These proper boundaries, however, are not altogether self-enforcing. They require support from intelligent political opinions. I discuss this issue in some of what follows.

MODERN AND CLASSIC VIRTUE

The characteristically modern virtues do not exhaust everything that moderns believe to be virtuous, for we also, by and large, find the classical virtues to be good. This excellence allows us to understand and pursue them, at least partially, and ultimately permits us to understand the nobility of, say, wisdom and justice on their own terms. Moreover, the (almost) independent attractiveness of a virtue such as full responsibility shades into classic virtue simply. Furthermore, virtues such as niceness and tolerance, as well as (energetic) industriousness and responsibility, shade into concepts and descriptions like gentleness, moderation, mildness, quickness, courage, and venturesomeness, that classically were subdivisions of virtue as a whole.[13] This suggests that while modern virtue is Lockean or Machiavellian, it nonetheless finally is explicable and understandable in classic terms. We must still recognize, however, that the flattening nature of liberal democracy affects our experience and public treatment of these classical virtues, as it does other goods.[14]

NOTES

1. Almost anyone who reads Aristotle's *Ethics* or Plato's dialogues is struck by how little has changed. The theoretical question is whether in discussing new

virtues modern thinkers simply add to, subtract from, or rename what Aristotle uncovers, without changing it fundamentally, or whether they grasp things differently at root. If the modern discussion of virtue is genuinely new, is this because the ancients failed to discover or account for phenomena that then formed the ground of modern virtues? Or is it because modern thought and opinion simply choose to emphasize the worth of things that the ancients understood, but evaluated differently? I will touch on this question at the end of the chapter.

2. In addition to the *Ethics,* the works of political philosophy that are most directly relevant for this chapter are Rousseau's *Second Discourse;* Locke's *Letter Concerning Toleration;* Locke's *Second Treatise of Government,* chapter 5, especially paragraph 34; *Federalist* 23, 63, 70, 77, 79; and Plato's *Statesman,* 305 E1-309 B8. Consider also Harvey C. Mansfield, Jr., *Taming the Prince* (New York: Free Press, 1987), 267; Harvey C. Mansfield, Jr., *America's Constitutional Soul* (Baltimore: Johns Hopkins University Press, 1991), 128–34, 216–19; and Leo Strauss, *Liberalism, Ancient and Modern* (New York: Basic Books, 1968).

3. What one "deserves" in modern life is, in a sense, an equal share of citizenship, rights, and opportunity: what one deserves is not some proper share as defined by a principle of distribution tied to substantive goods, such as honor or wealth. Even goods distributed more clearly according to talent—seats in, say, orchestras, colleges, and baseball dugouts—require training and effort, because to begin with these seats are open to all, and some who cannot make the team will, by a principle other than athletic excellence, eventually buy it. I discuss justice more completely in my chapter on law.

4. On compassion, see, among other articles by Clifford Orwin, his "Compassion and the Softening of Mores," *Journal of Democracy* (January 2000), 142–48.

5. For a discussion of the arguments supporting the idea of toleration in the "formative period" of this idea from the beginning of Protestantism through Locke and the Enlightenment, see Perez Zagorin, *How the Idea of Religious Toleration Came to the West* (Princeton, N.J.: Princeton University Press, 2003).

6. Consider Plato's *Statesman,* 260C-E.

7. Obviously, someone who works hard actually to complete his job well and not merely to work at it diligently needs something of the responsible man's total view. Moreover, although responsibility tends toward the comprehensive and even detached outlook that guides the completion of what is being done—the responsible man, as we said, sees to it that the job is done right—we initially consider responsibility to involve one's own "hands on" efforts. Industriousness in the full sense and responsibility in one common sense tend toward each other.

8. "Collective" responsibility is, therefore, not properly understood as either mysteriously historical and traditional or altogether meaningless. We to some degree cause acts of groups to which we choose to belong, or cause acts of others

that we could have prevented. In these (sometimes limited and, as we will see in the next chapter, hard to apportion) ways, collective responsibility is not an empty notion. One might consider Hannah Arendt, *Responsibility and Judgment* (New York: Schocken Books, 2003), and, more generally, Aristotle's discussion in the *Ethics* of matters that involve accountability.

9. Consider, among the several books and articles on responsibility, Hilary Bok, *Freedom and Responsibility* (Princeton, N.J.: Princeton University Press, 1998); J. R. Lucas, *Responsibility* (New York: Oxford University Press, 1993), and Jonathan Glover, *Responsibility* (New York: Humanities Press, 1970). On liberal virtues generally, consider William Galston, *Liberal Purposes* (Cambridge: Cambridge University Press, 1991), and Stephen Macedo, *Liberal Virtues* (New York: Oxford University Press, 1990).

10. Also in this sense we speak of our responsibilities, our jobs or tasks, as our "obligations," especially when we think of obligation simply as what we owe others and do not have a fancy theory of it.

11. I will add to my description of responsibility in the chapters that follow.

12. See *Federalist* 23, 63, 70, 77, 79. I discuss the practical reasoning involved in modern political responsibility more fully in the next chapter.

13. See Plato's *Statesman*, 305E1–309 B8.

14. Even responsibilities that some understand as religious duties are affected by belonging to modern responsibility and tolerance. If our obligations properly belong to free, equal, authoritative individuals, however, not religious subjects, this flattening is desirable, or necessary.

2

RESPONSIBILITY AND POLITICS

RESPONSIBILITY AND PUBLIC SERVICE

Responsibility is more than an individual virtue. It is central to the way our political institutions work and to their working well. I will examine political responsibility by discussing public service (or "bureaucracy"), then developing my analysis of limited government and political leadership, before turning in the next chapter to foreign affairs.

American government is the first modern government, so it makes sense that responsibility and other modern virtues fit our purposes and practices. This seems surprising only if, as often happens, we miss the link between virtue and self-interest.

To understand adequately responsibility's place in American politics we must begin with our founding purpose, which seems plain enough: to secure equally for all the natural rights to life, liberty, and the pursuit of happiness.[1] But what do we mean by natural rights? We think of rights as what we deserve. The right to a fair trial is an obvious example. This and similar examples (say, the "right" to employment and a certain income) lead us to think of rights as substantive guarantees. In the origins of liberalism and our constitution, however, rights involved chances, opportunities, or methods of access, not prescribed outcomes. This is evident in the right to obtain and hold property, to speak freely, to exercise one's religion, to pursue happiness, and even to have a fair trial. Fundamentally, a right is an authority to direct, determine, choose, pursue, act, possess, use, or enjoy. In Locke's theory of liberalism, moreover, and in the writings of Hobbes that preceded it, the true origin of rights is nature—hence, natural rights.[2] Nature here means two things, with neither element restricted to liberal political thought. First, something natural is what it is spontaneously, independent of creation or interference. We can see this if we look at our ordinary, everyday, commonsense conversation. In it we sometimes tell people to "be natural." We mean that they should be uncalculating, unforced, real, and not artificial or phony. In a word, they should be spontaneous. If we expand this notion all the way so that it does not refer just to this or that person or situation, we reach full spontaneity, full self-generation, full self-causality, dependency on nothing else. The fully natural is the fully spontaneous.

Second, nature means what is true of something generally or universally. Commonsensically, we often say when someone acts in a certain way—she is lazy, irresponsible, very precise, or messy—that it is her nature, that it is her dominant or pervasive characteristic. If we expand the notion of what is pervasive to its limit we reach the notion of what is fully universal—say, a natural law of physics. The fully natural is the fully universal.[3]

Taking rights and nature together, then, we see that natural rights are the authorities for choice that cover every authority to choose and that exist spontaneously, whatever we do, however we change things and make them over. In the liberal understanding, natural rights belong to individuals, and they belong to each of us equally. Individuals are those who in a spontaneous way own (and therefore deserve) the authority to direct, determine, choose, act, pursue, possess, use or enjoy, and this root authority covers all people and all choices equally.[4]

The second central element of liberalism concerns this question: Who exactly is the naturally authoritative individual? Hobbes and Locke talk of the centrality of self-preservation—and ultimately of comfortable self-preservation. Hobbes also talks of the fear of violent death. He sees other desires in its light.[5] What does it mean to flee from death and satisfy the desire for self-preservation? For liberal thinkers, to satisfy desire is to quell uneasiness.[6] Fleeing death is fleeing the void, nothing, emptiness. So, what Hobbes and Locke ultimately mean is that what motivates natural individuals is the restless movement from nothing in particular to nothing in particular, with various arbitrary resting points along the way. The self is this movement and resting, and the calculation and control appropriate to them. Happiness is not fulfillment oriented to set ends. Rather, it is the accumulation of variable satisfactions that are stopping points from which one gathers energy for continued movement. What is good for me is whatever I judge will keep my restless motion going, perpetually.

A third basic element of liberalism concerns the status of property, or power. Property, one's private substance, becomes central because it is the neutral good we can use to satisfy any desire. The liberal self's wish to continue its restless activity is in practice largely satisfied by the movement of accumulating and acquiring power generally and property in particular—not so much spending and employing as obtaining and holding. Acquisition is not primarily about enjoyment but about the increasingly controlled and energetic movement away from death and unease.

A fourth central element of liberalism is the importance of freedom. If we examine our uses of "free," we see that freedom generally means to be unconstrained or uncontrolled, to not be stopped or pushed. (Prisoners are "freed," i.e., no longer locked up; slaves are forced or ordered by others.)[7] To be free is to be self-directed and not hindered in the movement or action of that direction. Lack of constraint and control, however, have no developed meaning except together with that from which one is (not) held back or to which one is (not) pushed.[8] Liberal freedom is to be self-directed and unconstrained in satisfying desires for objects ("interests") that are in principle equal. It is not identical to freedom simply but has a specific kind of neutrality, poised attention, and movement that differ from freedom connected to enjoyment otherwise understood.[9] In our contemporary liberal sense, freedom is a flat uninvolvement, a being left alone, in relation to which any possible flatly desired interest or good can then be pursued and the means toward it found. Such freedom is analogous to property as we just described it—a generally useful good or characteristic not tied to especially uplifting desires.[10]

The effort to secure the sway of natural rights and liberties and to expand their exercise encourages energetic self-interest. We use our liberty to satisfy the desires that we, not others, choose and to accumulate the property that enables us to do this successfully.[11] A

country such as ours that secures such sway comes in turn to depend on the self-interest it encourages, primarily as an energetic
spirit of acquisition. Such a country also relies on citizens who support self-government limited by its service to individual interest or
right, to its protection and promotion of "life, liberty and the pursuit of happiness." No authorities but we ourselves can defend us le-
gitimately.

In light of our previous considerations, we may combine these
traits of private and public spirit and conclude that the purpose of our
politics is to foster the education and actions of responsible individuals. Our reigning standpoint is the virtue of the free self who considers his interests in the longer term; it is not self-interest as immediate
satisfaction.[12] Because responsible individuals often flourish more im-
pressively outside government than in it, moreover, and are less defined by specific activities than are men devoted to classic virtue or
faith, the link between who governs (and how) and their ends is more
obscure in liberal democracies than in other regimes. This is one reason why the tie between our virtues and our self-interest is easy to
miss.[13] Nonetheless, the link exists, and I will assert in this chapter that
good government in America—government that serves worthwhile
purposes in a worthwhile way—is essentially responsible government,
properly understood. Responsible representatives and bureaucrats
help to achieve the purpose of the American regime and, at the same
time, exemplify the actions and limits of responsible individualism.

Unattractive Responsibility

Whatever good things we may say about responsibility, we also
should recognize what is dull and ponderous about it. Who wants to
spend the weekend with someone famous for his responsibility? Being responsible means not having fun. Acting responsibly means not
doing as you would like. Responsibility is a sober characteristic that
we all may grudgingly respect but that only a teenager's father could
love. Concern with it is chief among the traits that make fathers seem
heavy-handed, old-fashioned, humorless, and overbearing in the few
moments they do not seem bumbling, woebegone, hapless, and out of
touch.

To add to the unattractiveness, the public search for the responsible figure is usually the search for someone to blame, not praise. "Who is responsible?" means "Whom can I punish?" Not a day goes by in which congressmen are not planning or holding hearings to fix responsibility, so that they may destroy careers and reputations, or at least make someone suffer. After all, if they cannot find someone else accountable for the September 11 attacks or for failed intelligence before the Iraq War, then perhaps we will say that they themselves are accountable; at the least, they seem irresponsible if they do not live up to their "oversight" responsibility.

Being responsible seems boring and assigning accountability mean-spirited. We rarely think it vicious, of course, but displaying and demanding it often is narrow-minded and occasionally hypocritical. Yet unattractive as responsibility may appear, consider what we think of politicians and bureaucrats. Many think elected officials are finger-pointing, blame-dodging, money-wasting, unprincipled scoundrels. "Bureaucrat" is a word to which "petty" attaches itself as surely as rubber is glued to stamp: Government officials, we so often believe, are narrow-minded, small-souled, officious, inflexible, rule-mongering, paper-chasing weasels. Coupling responsibility with bureaucracy may mean that the weasel no longer fecklessly whistles while he works, or that he blames himself for losing your license application rather than scolding you for asking about it, but the coupling of bureaucracy and responsibility is hardly the exciting marriage of the century.

Scholarly Responsibility

It might therefore come as a surprise that properly defining and institutionalizing political and, especially, bureaucratic responsibility was for many years among political scientists almost synonymous with good government.[14] Academics thought that bureaucracy was indispensable for modern life, but ordinary citizens thought that it often was undemocratic. Political scientists, therefore, needed to show how it could be democratic after all. "Not only must we reject the idea that democracy is opposed to bureaucracy," wrote a young political scientist who later was to become a dean of his profession, but we must recognize that the future of democracy depends upon its ability to maintain a fully organized bureaucracy. For the industrial system which demands it is with us for better or worse since the life of millions of human beings depends upon it. If a popular government is incapable of maintaining a bureaucratic hierarchy, it is bound to give way to a form of government which will accomplish that, whether it be the dictatorship of an individual or of a small group in the name of the nation, the people, or the proletariat.[15]

In order to show how bureaucracy could be democratic, political scientists considered how to make it responsible. For, by democracy they largely had in mind representative democracy; by representation they largely had in mind responding to popular interests; and by responsibility they almost exclusively had in mind accountability. If the people and their representatives could hold bureaucrats to account in serving their interests, then bureaucracy and democracy could be reconciled.

This was and is a difficult task, for several reasons. Bureaucrats might have professional or scientific skills that make them hard to control and understand; indeed, it often is their expertise that makes them useful in the first place. They might follow procedures with such scrupulous (or unthinkingly lazy) precision that they are beyond the reach of valid individual adjustments and exceptions; in fact, it is only by carefully following rules that they can deal with great complexity and large numbers quickly and fairly. They might have selfish interests that are easy to mask in a civil service system with weak internal controls and little professional esprit de corps. Also, they might be practicing in an administration with such unclear direction that there is little to which to hold them to account. Indeed, they might be practicing in a constitutional regime, such as ours, that appears designed always to check and frustrate clear direction.

The result of these possibilities is that bureaucrats seem to have less accountability and more free rein—to be used lazily, automatically, venally, or in pursuit of their own sense of what is best—than is democratically healthy.

Scholars invented remedies for these ills. They asked civil servants to be accountable to professional norms, to take sophisticated views of their jobs, and to involve in their work local groups of interested citizens. They argued the importance of budget and personnel staffs that would speak to each other across the government and allow mature coordination and control. Above all, they sought ways to turn elections into obvious referenda on policies and programs, so that the president and Congress would be more accountable to the people, less at odds with each other, and more easily able to control administrators. The high point of this effort was an explosion of support for doctrines of "responsible" party government that in different degrees tried to assimilate America's Constitution to Britain's practices by subordinating to political parties with precisely defined programs both the separation of powers and the individual accountability of representatives to their constituents. "Party government would establish popular control over government by making the group of rulers in power *collectively* responsible to the people."[16]

Not all scholars and journalists made these arguments, of course, and several wrote against them. But the thrust was that modern life needs bureaucracy and that bureaucrats need to be responsible. Such arguments and concerns remain relevant. We still worry that bureaucracies are heavy-handed and unresponsive, although we also are troubled when they deviate unfairly from standard procedures and give some people special privileges. Also, although technology and the judiciary are today's focus of our greatest concerns about irresponsible expertise, the conflicts between bureaucratic expertise and accountability remain vivid. The classic problem of the tension between the (possible and sought after) wisdom of the governors and the (necessary) consent of the governed cannot help but appear everywhere.

That said, today's immediate debate about bureaucrats has more to do with the government's size—with whether bureaucrats should act at all—than with how they can act more responsibly. Today's discussion of responsibility concerns the "personal" responsibility of, say, unwed mothers and absent fathers as much as political accountability. The crux of contemporary debate concerns more what government should do than how it can be more responsive. To discuss the issue of political and bureaucratic responsibility with greater acuity, therefore, we need to relate the problem of responsibility in, of, and for government to broader questions of the purpose, connection to character, and scope of liberal democracy. We began this discussion in the previous chapter and at the start of this one. The heart of responsibility is more than the spirit of accountability: it is to do one's own job effectively and to take charge of common tasks that belong to no one in particular. I will now develop more directly the constitutional implications of this view.

Representatives' Responsibility

In the United States we promote political responsibility and responsible individuals through a government that we form constitutionally. If we reflect carefully on this familiar observation, we will be able to understand political and bureaucratic responsibility better, by putting them in a broader political frame.

The Constitution seeks to advance equal liberty by assuring as best it can that those who govern deliberate on many measures, but for limited purposes. To do this it looks to popular interests while also controlling possible majority tyranny, and it employs individual judgment and energy while limiting overweening individuals or dominating minority factions. It must divide and domesticate, but not eliminate, the proud and the able; it must disperse and redirect, but not eradicate, the narrowly self-interested and cunning.

We see best how the American founders effected their intention by considering separation of powers. Separation of powers means dispersal of government power among offices. The people rule indirectly through representatives, who work through offices that they fill in different ways and times. Functions are not simply split, however, so that, for example, only one set of officials deals with financial or foreign affairs. Rather, no office totally controls any issue, several offices have some effect on many issues, and a few affect all. Offices' range, quality, and immediacy of impact do not vary randomly, however, but in ways connected to the Constitution's statement of their size, length of term, and powers. The complexity and interplay among offices make it difficult for anyone (including a majority of the people) to have his (or its) way directly and completely.

These apparently mechanical structures of separated powers come to life in two ways. One is through respect or reverence for the Constitution itself, for the form engendered by the founders' understanding and intentions.[17] This respect is not merely ceremonial. On the contrary, we embody it in our practice as ordinary citizens, namely, in the unusual degree to which we obey results of duly constituted forms for choice—elections, juries, presidential directives, congressional deliberations, and votes—even when they thwart our immediate desires. This devotion is much more remarkable than we usually recognize.

Respect for constitutional results does not determine their full substance, of course, although it limits the ordinary range of possibilities. Rather, the impetus for action comes from the variety of interests, opinions, and passions that government represents and that the separation of powers organizes with subtlety and complexity. Here, structure comes to life through the deliberation and persuasion that occur because our representatives, separated into their official responsibilities, take their jobs seriously, as we expect them to. Attachment to their offices and attention to their range, powers, and purposes enables representatives to bring to bear a variety of immediate and extended considerations.[18] When separation of powers works best, legislative compromise occurs in which representatives discover commonly acceptable solutions to generally perceived problems, and executive enterprise occurs in which representatives deal with wars or other direct threats; with circumstances that require congealed interests to be relaxed and overcome (as Franklin Roosevelt or Ronald Reagan acted to rescue or resuscitate economic enterprise); or with situations (such as the one Lincoln faced) that demand uncommon education, risk, far-sightedness, and invention to protect rights or to restore them.[19]

When representatives attach actions to offices they are carrying out their constitutional responsibilities. When citizens attach interests to voting and respecting constitutional outcomes, they are carrying out theirs. Doing one's job responsibly is not equivalent to the immediate responsiveness of representatives to citizens (or of a citizen to his own most immediate desires), because to serve interests successfully is not always to do what people want immediately. Moreover, even reasonable accountability differs among officeholders, because we judge them through different elections. We hold them to account for different interests and for measures that secure these interests over different terms. Senators, for example, as Madison argues in *Federalist* 63, deal with objectives that depend "on a succession of well-chosen and well-connected measures, which have a gradual and perhaps unobserved operation." They act responsibly when they pursue such objectives successfully. By implication, senators should perform this long-term job even if people often hold them to account irresponsibly.

The matter is still more complex. Because every congressional vote reflects a clash of long and short-term interests and objectives, it often seems that no representative does just what the people want.[20] By doing his job responsibly each representative may look as if he has failed. This is still another reason why assuming responsibility must go beyond fearing accountability, and why electorates should learn to respect thoughtful representatives and not just those who appear to satisfy them immediately.

This difficulty of assigning accountability indicates how even responsibility as doing one's job sometimes falls short. Why should any citizen pay attention to the common interest, or stand for election, if immediate self-interest does not require it? Why, having chosen to stand for election, should he risk the wrath of his constituents by "failing" them in favor of what is responsible over the long term? Whatever other motives may exist, responsibly assuming the tasks that are no one's and everyone's is necessary to serve common interests well. Respect or responsibility for the whole is at some point indispensable.

Because our Constitution encourages natural political spirit to satisfy itself through partial responsibilities that belong to a deliberative whole, and because it encourages (and almost forces) interests we satisfy in common (say, through legislation) to attend to complex governmental responsibilities and their results, the Constitution helps to produce these very characteristics it needs, even apart from the measures we pass and enforce, and from private education and professional behavior.[21] When, for example, I cannot satisfy my selfish desire to protect my property without the public protection of laws and police, and when the interest I share with others to establish an effective police power bears fruit only after extensive deliberation and discussion, the habit of respecting and attending to others' interests and of delaying or foregoing my own immediate satisfaction (through, say, crime) increases and grows. At the same time, this respect for others and for what is common is built on the solid foundation of individual rights and interests. Similarly, when my desire to acquire and enjoy goods is deflected from crime and easy satisfaction toward the regulated competition of markets, the spirit of acquisition begins to be expanded and enhanced at the very moment it is frustrated, and the overall wealth that it creates is increased. In the same way, by giving natural political spirit so many opportunities for private enterprises and public office, the Constitution both calls it forth and limits it. The Constitution thus frustrates the tendency of any spirit to dominate yet allows and even encourages all to be more responsible, subtle, and complex; in this way it expands self-government generally.[22] The Constitution at once requires, stimulates, and limits citizens' assumption of visible, and ultimately more remote, public responsibilities that belong to no one in particular.

I will sum up these reflections as follows. Elected representatives' accountability to the people derives from the respect citizens and representatives have for elections, offices, and other constitutional forms. These forms and respect are allied to the goal of securing individual rights and to liberating a widespread spirit of economic acquisition and self-rule. We discover the measures that secure rights and enhance public and private spirit through legislative and executive deliberation, compromise, and enterprise as these qualities are dispersed and called forth in a variety of positions. The clash among representatives who are accountable to voters at different places and times and who have different and often loosely defined ranges of political control brings about results that generally serve these purposes. Actually accomplishing one's job, loosely defined as this job sometimes is (rather than merely accepting blame for failure or defensively creating a record of consultation), being accountable by respecting the electoral limits and source of one's office (rather than by instantly bowing to constituents' immediate interests), and, as much as one can, attending to remote and long-term considerations is what constitutes the true responsibility of representatives, and their genuine responsiveness.[23] By taking on public tasks that belong to them no more than to any other citizen, moreover, and by working in terms of (rather than outside of) a constitutional separation of powers that both frustrates and energizes them, representatives display and develop some of the controlled spirit (i.e., some of the character) the liberation and enhancement of which is a goal of the measures they enact.

Bureaucratic Responsibility

These accounts of responsibility and its constitutional framework help us see more subtly than before the link between responsibility and public service. Turning to bureaucracy, I will argue that true bureaucratic responsibility is not immediate accountability to the whims of superiors or the electorate.[24] Nor is it bowing to or recklessly implementing some abstract professional or moral standard. Nor, moreover, is it doing one's job mechanically or defensively with little attention to actual results or to whether these results in fact serve citizens' purposes and interests. Rather, bureaucratic responsibility is an attenuated version of the more subtle and complex responsibility of representatives that I have just discussed. It is attenuated because for most bureaucrats the job and the guidance from superiors are more narrow and direct than they are for most representatives. The problem of bureaucratic responsibility, therefore, is not as fundamental as the question of the responsibility of representatives, but it is not different in kind.[25]

I begin by noting and modifying the usual view of bureaucracy, turning next to the limits of bureaucratic accountability for controlling bureaucratic failings, and concluding with a summary statement.

The picture-book portrait of "bureaucracy" depicts an organization that works by following public rules designed to treat each case identically, employing many officials who perform precise tasks within a precise hierarchical structure. The Social Security Administration is a good example. The virtue of such organizations is to do a large amount of business fairly and reasonably, using a division of labor that allows much that we discover technologically to become economically and militarily useful.[26]

The government agencies that we see around us, however, vary in many ways from this picture. A good public school, for example, treats everyone equally, but only up to the point where differences in talent demand differences in approach; pays as much attention to what works in educating students here and now as it does to pedagogical "rules"; uses employees (teachers) who perform countless tasks directed to whole children, not narrow tasks directed to parts; and is not especially hierarchical. Most actual public schools are at least as close to this picture as to the standard bureaucratic one (and most likely closer to it).[27] For bureaucracies such as schools, tasks and methods are variegated and complex. We require them to be responsible, but with so much complexity accountability becomes hard to judge. Worse, if responsibility comes merely to mean being accountable for rules and being blameworthy for deviating from them, it is harmful. For schools learn to avoid blame (and therefore reduce their effectiveness) by having every teacher follow the same strict procedure for every student. We wish teachers to pay actual attention to their students' success—because of these teachers' skill, self-reliance, dependability, pride, and competition with peers (i.e., because of elements of responsibility)—rather than having the kind of "democratic" accountability in which everyone looks over everyone else's shoulder.

Hidden Responsibility

Another reason why the standpoint of effectiveness rather than of such accountability is necessary for democratic bureaucrats is because they do much that is hidden from public view and timely judgment. Who, for example, can measure the exact contribution of State Department diplomacy toward defeating Soviet communism during the 1980s? Perhaps the discipline and foresight of the Defense Department was decisive. Perhaps the sheer volume and tenacity of the Reagan military buildup was central, largely independent of how well the Pentagon handled it. That is, perhaps President Reagan, or Defense Secretary Caspar Weinberger, or the senators they convinced, or the American people who elected them were more significant than any bureaucrat in any department. Yet, perhaps technology was more decisive than any contribution of management or politics; perhaps the power of liberty and of those who died, or even argued, for it was more significant still. Or perhaps Soviet leaders simply lost their will.

If we narrow the example to more concrete policies, it is easier to assign accountability. It was particular diplomats (and not others) who, for example, met with colleagues in Italy in 1983 to persuade them to stand firm on NATO's wish to locate intermediate-range missiles there, and certain colonels and generals, not others, who grasped the capabilities of such missiles and planned to produce and buy them. Their steadfastness marked for the Soviets new, visible American resolve.[28] Yet, countless other people in the State Department, Pentagon, and on congressional staffs contributed to this success—or impeded it. How many of them were properly recognized or reprimanded? More, how could one tell how much this single policy affected matters, compared to everything that happened before or after? Whether people are doing their job, how much this job contributes to the result, how much the result contributes to the larger aim, and how sensible the aim is in the first place—all this often is obscure.[29] Even assessments of the government's antiterror performance prior to the September 11 attacks lay surprisingly few critical actions at the feet of particular officials in particular times and places.[30] In any event, perhaps it was less these actions and inactions than a general lack of timely information and cooperation that caused opportunities to be missed.

In addition to hiddenness or obscurity, and to the prevalence of bureaucracies that deal more with individual cases than with rules, a third limit to the democratic accountability of bureaucrats is the openness of bureaucratic tasks. Many bureaucracies have at least some elements of what we have described in schools. Usually, the lower one goes in most organizations, the narrower and more defined the job. A clerk in the Justice Department performs more circumscribed tasks than the attorney general. Sometimes, however, even those far enough down the hierarchy to be directly in the line of fire—a policeman walking the beat, say—have jobs that are not very well circumscribed.[31]

One's initial reaction to this problem might be to define jobs better by writing exhaustive job descriptions and sets of rules to cover every possible engagement. But ill-defined jobs sometimes have large aims—preventing crime, keeping immediate peace, educating children, promoting national security—that are not well met by limiting the job precisely, narrowly, and restrictively—that is, "bureaucratically." Sometimes, too much depends on connections among nebulous aims and complex circumstances—what counts as peace or calm, for example; for how long this calm must be kept; who causes the danger; what one's immediate resources are—for restrictive definitions to allow jobs to be done effectively. Other times—in genuine education, again—liberty of action is inherent in reaching the goal and in the good itself. Not everything can be reduced to precise rules in order to control precise activities that are precise means to precise ends.

How does responsibility help to relieve these difficulties? The hiddenness of much that bureaucrats do and the flexibility of their tasks mean that we cannot ensure through close control that everyone does his job well. Even if we could, we want bureaucrats to do even visible and narrow jobs effectively—that is, in a way that takes special circumstances into account and therefore requires some freedom from following precise rules. Occasionally, latecomers to the Motor Vehicle Bureau do need to be put at the head of the line. Fear of punishment (assuming we could observe better and wish to control more rigidly) will not produce sufficient energy and innovation among public servants, useful as it might be for limiting corruption.

Rather than fear and close control, what appears necessary is to encourage bureaucrats to do their duty, perform their obligations, and act on the basis of decent habits, friendship, and loyalty. Friendship and loyalty are insufficient in bureaucracies, however, because so many organizations have such changeable membership.[32] Also, although good work because of duty and obligation surely is desirable, "duty" points to subservience to an occupational, professional, religious, or moral code that is either narrower or broader than service in the public interest in liberal democracies. Our bureaucracies usually are composed of people who are present voluntarily, with entrance and exit governed by contract, ambition, and economic opportunity more than by tradition or attachment to land and family. As we have argued, responsibility is the virtue that speaks to the necessity and desirability of duty in a way that captures the peculiar quality of modernity and its purposes, in which obligations, friendships, and professions all are in the last analysis chosen voluntarily to serve energetic, acquisitive individuals. To be responsible is to do one's job well not because of inherited attachments but within a structure of rights, common tasks, and interests. It is to succeed when one's job could be someone (or anyone) else's. It is fostering this element of responsibility, more than mechanisms to improve immediate accountability, that is crucial to meeting bureaucracies' weaknesses and to ensuring that public servants are effective.

Conclusion

I conclude my reflections on bureaucracy and responsibility as follows. Public servants should be responsible, but this must mean more than being transparently accountable to the people and their representatives, and it rarely means being directly accountable to an extraconstitutional order or to a professional code of practices and principles.[33] Rather, it involves the understanding of responsibility I have been discussing, a sense that defines the responsibility of citizens and political representatives as well as of bureaucrats, a sense that is specified by characteristics that are at once means and ends of our regime. The responsibility we need from the public servant is that he actually does his own job, as effectively as he can. Sometimes this means that he exercises a freedom that seems too unregulated or even seeks to expand his responsibilities beyond what his job appears to require. The teacher who attends to each student differently might be too harsh with some and too easy with others. The State Department official negotiating one element of an arms treaty may see and seize opportunities to redirect, say, nuclear proliferation policy more generally than his brief stipulates. The government attorney who is writing an equal opportunity regulation may have in mind a result that will affect agencies other than his own. The check on such liberty must be others' exercising their own liberty, citizens at the polls or in the courts, fellow bureaucrats, and, above all, political executives. The spirit of responsibility cannot be restricted mechanically to mere dependability any more than it can be captured through narrow accountability, for it often seeks new areas over which to take charge. Indeed, this connection of responsibility to effectiveness more than to guilt makes it difficult to specify precisely or universally what all responsibility requires. The variety of tasks, abilities, and lengths and breadths of view means that we cannot ask each public servant, or everyone simply, to be equally responsible. To do so limits what is best in it.[34]

Because so many bureaucracies live or attempt to live by the identical application of rules, they too often are dominated by an ethic of narrow accountability rather than effective responsibility. This problem is somewhat offset by the difficulties in assigning accountability and by the competition among public servants who deal with similar issues, a competition that brings out responsibility in the more effective sense. Of course, however responsible bureaucrats may be, all but those at the very top are constrained by the actions and responsibilities of political executives. They depend in the end on the effectiveness of representatives, and the people. However much government's laws and measures may in turn influence this effectiveness, respect for the Constitution itself, and for the scope of private liberty, shapes it still more.

RESPONSIBILITY AND LIMITED GOVERNMENT

I am arguing that responsible bureaucracies are effective ones and that in responsible action generally the spirit of success differs from the spirit of narrow, immediate, rule-based, guilt-fearing accountability. Responsible government is energized by individual effectiveness. No automatic working of institutions can guarantee this, and excessive accountability corrupts it.

This argument is, on its face, at odds with limited government. I intend now to explore limited government and politics more fully by turning from the restricted responsibility of bureaucrats to the broader responsibilities of executives and legislators.

However fluid the tasks of bureaucrats, their jobs are reasonably well restricted and defined: teach this class, walk this beat, process these forms. But what exactly are the responsibilities of legislators, of the "chief executive," and of the executives who control bureaucracies? They take on the larger tasks that belong to no one in particular. What can count as effective action, however, when assignments seemingly are so amorphous? Knowing how to achieve a result is sometimes connected to a public servant's professional knowledge or technical skill. Through what knowledge, however, do we responsibly balance and choose the ends themselves? Indeed, how do we intelligently select and deploy the methods to implement these ends when (as is often the case) the means are controversial? These questions are not themselves matters of professional skill, science, or technique, I will argue, but of the combined knowledge and disposition involved in responsible action or in virtue generally. I will discuss this practical (as opposed to theoretical, professional, traditional, or moralistic) knowledge and action by developing my earlier remarks about enterprise and compromise.[35]

Enterprise and Compromise

Enterprise and compromise are the core of responsible political action. They are the ways we understand and carry out tasks that affect everyone, require (some) common effort, and could by right be done by anyone. As is true of responsibility, tolerance, industriousness, and being "nice," they are characteristics newly described or valued in modern life. Being willing to compromise can be synonymous with being nice, undemanding, or tolerant. Just as one can be too nice, one can be too compromising, a compromiser, or find oneself in a compromising position. Here one gives away or is forced to give away too much of one's own or one's trustees' interests. The special meaning of compromise that differentiates it from being nice generally arises when we must achieve our interests together with others; compromise is the characteristic that allows us to see (and rest on) ground where we can pursue our interests in tandem. It is a disposition activated and directed by one's responsibilities; as is true of responsibility generally, it can stretch beyond one's immediate tasks.

Being "enterprising" can be synonymous with being industrious or hard working. We (sometimes ironically) praise someone for being enterprising in small things, such as attacking the overgrown lawn or cleaning the overstuffed garage. The special quality of enterprise even in such small things is to begin on one's own, charge ahead energetically to finish things off (and not only to do things step by step), look for new ways to do the job, and then search for and find new things to do. In this way enterprise can move from self-initiating energy that disposes of what is in front of one to ways, means, innovations, inventions, and tasks that are novel, bold, or risky. Enterprise is modern in its breadth (one can be enterprising about anything from developing land to conglomerating television stations, to producing plays); in the fact that although it has elements of courage, ambition, and pride, it is too general and inventive to be identical to these virtues; and in the poetic shaping or imperial reach one sometimes sees in the grandest enterprises.

Although spirit and the thrill of risk can support enterprise, to be enterprising is a disposition, not a passion. It is a disposition to excess when more concerned with display than results, but virtuous when linked to responsible success (i.e., to stable success connected to equal freedom in pursuing self-interest). It can work together with and help impel a responsible man's move to greater and greater fields. It satisfies less by seeing new ways to meet old interests than by (at least somewhat) transforming interests and needs so we see them in a new light. At its best, enterprise is linked to responsibility as far-sighted boldness that seeks to expand and accomplish its tasks on the basis of responsibly attending to (taking charge of) one's own and others' futures.

Enterprise, Compromise, and Political Responsibility

Let me now consider more directly how enterprise and compromise work with the responsibilities of office, considering executive action first. What is central here is to grasp the essentially political (and not "administrative") nature of government. Those with bureaucratic responsibilities function best within well-directed agencies guided by political executives. Even officials who require latitude take their lead from heads, because, on the whole, some degree of hierarchy prevails. More often than not, officials try to do what they are told. They must be told, however, and the teller must manifestly believe what he says. Bureaucrats and others constantly pepper agency heads with suggestions that they often describe as requirements and necessities. It is only on the basis of self-confidence that an executive can accept or reject these demands intelligently.[36]

The confident self-assertion and steadfastness successfully displayed by heads, and their subordinates' voluntary loyalty and obedience, are the first elements of the essentially practical (as opposed to technical and narrowly moral) atmosphere of government action. The executive's self-confidence and steadfastness in turn make evident an important link between responsibility and enterprise. For, administrations and bureaucracies that work well are headed by those alive to the undefined substance of their tasks. To serve in government is to be constantly amazed by how much is there for the taking, how little anyone knows about what should be done or who should do it. An executive agency with a confident head can accomplish things in areas where it hardly seems to belong. Risk and enterprise, shaping situations, shifting and defining terms of debate, seeing others' viewpoints as mere hills and valleys in a landscape of one's own design—these are the characteristics of an executive who does his job.

Responsibility favors and often requires self-propelled boldness or, at least, redefinition, if it is to succeed. A list of effective presidents and cabinet heads almost always centers on actions they took that are of this sort. Current examples abound, ranging from President Clinton's redirecting the connection between welfare and work through President Reagan's forming foreign policy by looking back from the then only imagined American victory in the Cold War, to Mayor Giuliani's unsentimental view of crime in New York City and how best to prevent it.[37] One also could explore in these terms Reagan's tax policies, the ebb and flow of power in such agencies as the Federal Drug Administration, the creation of metropolitan New York's parks and parkways, the place of state attorneys general in dealing with national issues of health and finance, and countless other events.[38] Many more distant examples are equally telling.

The Political Reasoning of Executives

We can further understand enterprise (and responsibility generally) by considering more explicitly the kind and direction of reasoning it involves. An executive's characteristic political-ethical thinking always considers first what "feels" right to him. This means that the better choice is a course of action he can traverse spontaneously, using ways and means that come naturally. (An abstractly superior way is inferior if he is distracted by always looking at his feet or re-memorizing his lines.) His reasoning then considers who is for something and who is against it, and looks at how to deal with this person or that, here and now or then or there. The goal is to influence or persuade, and the question is what will get the persuading job done. Political-ethical reasoning is connected to action, and it is particular.

Most significantly, this reasoning is connected to the future, not just because its goal is a new effect but because the responsible executive always considers or intuits how matters will be transformed by his actions, how the second and third steps will occur in situations changed by his earlier measures. The political reasoning I have in mind considers in advance the reaction of opponents not only as they are now but also as they will become after things change. This especially is the reasoning that goes with responsible enterprise, which does not take thoughtless risks but looks back from the future and sees how friends, foes, and means of persuasion will appear on the path to, and as they are changed by this new point of view. "Visionary" rhetoric has its place here. Such practical reasoning, finally, is not a playbook, method, or step-by-step plan but, rather, what gives form and (constant) guidance to the enterprise, and, therefore, to such plans, which the executive also may be skilled in formulating.

In general, the successful executive takes his bearings less from given situations than from the future he would like to see. He is not guided by a here and now defined by others, and he does not conceive his task to be managing what others present him. Rather, he understands the current situation as a novel set of problems and opportunities leading to the future he has projected. Because he is practical, he attends carefully to the immediate constellation of interests and forces. Yet he does so primarily from the perspective of his own intentions, not the perspective of others' self-understanding, and he concentrates most on the new organization of interests and forces that will be shaped by each of his actions. Skillful subordinates are important, but loyalty, friendship, and trust are more decisive than competence.

The successful executive is most at home in an atmosphere of battle, challenge, new beginning, revival, and enterprise. His characteristic projection of novel possibilities and standpoints leads him to create this atmosphere even where it is not commonly recognized or desired. Ultimately the fullest examples of this type tend to seek for themselves an admiration that goes beyond mere respect for a job well done, however vast the job. Their way of seeing and acting so persistently from their own viewpoints leads followers and observers to attribute to them outstanding, even uncanny, qualities.

Something of this enterprising character belongs to every successful political executive; all discharge their responsibilities with a view to placing themselves in a larger field and putting others there with them. Indeed, some degree of the characteristic reasoning and forward-looking shaping we see in responsible enterprise may be necessary to succeed even in one's basic tasks. The responsibility of smaller and more usual executives seems to have a more defined purpose, however, so their political projections are held in check.

The Political Reasoning of Legislators

From where do the purposes and tasks of ordinary and more unusual executives arise? When linked to liberal democracy, the tasks are characteristically modern. Enterprise and loyalty are directed toward battles against drugs, crime, "dependence," recession, and inflation, and, of course, terrorists, fascists, and communists. In general, and certainly for bureaucratic executives, the purposes do not involve a massive new sense of the world and its working. Rather, the flat familiarity and multiplicity of the objects of desire that are liberated by the pursuit of happiness by and large remain the horizon of modern political action. This horizon helps contain bold executive action within responsible ends and tasks. What is characteristic of most political executives is to confront a public problem visible enough that all may validate it as a possibly proper object of limited government. They then understand and seek to resolve their problem, win their battle, or attain their purpose through some version of the bold, fluid, redefining ways I am discussing.

In practice, the smaller and even some of the larger purposes are given to executives by (or together with) legislators. It is important that we see how responsible legislators also are radically political in their thinking and acting.

A legislature such as ours is a living forge of consent. It represents individuals where their individual choices result in common situations that none would select.[39] Some believe it possible to discover or imagine what deserves to win uniform consent and therefore to do away with legislatures altogether. In actual politics however, we cannot allow the public exercise of individual rights to occur in this imaginary way. Our distrust of expert judgment would be deservedly well placed. Moreover, arriving at consensus is an exercise of freedom that belongs to the desirable expansion of responsibility. Others can never make a perfect decision for us if doing things for ourselves—*self*-government—is one of our goals. Actual consent is therefore necessary in liberal democracy. We must, however, find a way to allow intelligent public choice to occur where needed and to win consent to the choices actually made. Election by the people of those they think wise enough to represent them is the practical solution. Actually making and obeying laws is the lifeblood of the American regime.

Whereas the successful executive must win victories in larger and larger fields to satisfy his entrepreneurial self-confidence and win renown for his vigor and presence, the successful congressman or legislator makes himself and others content. Legislative parties may seek and win victories when they are part of the president's team, but left to their own devices legislators search for solutions about which no one complains too much. The legislator sees others' points of view—indeed, all points of view. He is responsibly fair-minded and temperate. He does not redefine contexts so much as he attempts to please all within a context he thinks of as permanent, or too difficult to change.

The effective legislator is as political in his thinking and acting as the effective executive. He too considers concrete interests and wishes in the here and now, and he thinks about how they can seem to be satisfied by his programs. He too always looks toward what can gain this or that person's support and cajoles or persuades with the tools that work in the given case. He too does not weigh abstract "values" to reach a decision or treat others as if they have unchangeable positions that reflect abstract desires but, rather, considers and strives for his purpose in ways closely tied to the immediate, specific, context within which he works. He too treats others as if they can be changed, but in a peculiar way. Unlike the successful executive, the legislator does not project a possibility in which he sees people and things in a new light. He does not redefine and reorient. Rather, he discovers largely conventional solutions to commonly defined problems and understands how the new situation, the compromise that he discerns, can be made attractive to people in terms of their immediate self-understanding. He projects areas of agreement under the current terms of debate and sees how the interests of those who must consent to a new law will look under the circumstances the new law creates. Although the executive also may begin from current concerns, one measure of his ability is his capacity to lead others to begin to grasp and articulate their concerns in his new terms, or at least to discover a wish in others that overrides their immediate desires and calculations. The measure of the legislator's ability, however, is his capacity to bring about a satisfactory result, still in the old terms. Whereas President Reagan finally succeeded in making us at once both conservative and entrepreneurial, his legislative team and Senate Majority Leader Dole needed to discover how to pass Reagan's tax cut before so many became Reaganites.[40] In general, then, the responsible legislator's gift is to fashion and effect compromise, while the executive's gift is to construct and lead a striking enterprise.

Executive and Legislative Responsibility

Needless to say, neither type is confined fully to one branch, and few individuals of either type are completely effective. These general characteristics and their paler imitations, however, help explain the push and pull of everyday politics. Our next task is to explore how executive energy and legislative action work to keep each other responsible.

One might imagine that legislators' caution or the clash of multiple executives is harmful. Why not complete executive dominance or monarchy? Executive rule by one or a few is dangerous because it is liable to arbitrary choice and adventurism. The possibility of popular consent would become increasingly trivial and remote were everything merely an element in some leader's master plan.

On the other hand, representative government often must step away from the immediate interests of people, because members of a liberal populace tend irresponsibly to seek individual advantage before they resign themselves to the need to secure a common benefit. Executives are best able to take this step. If the step is too fast and far, however, the government's measures will be uselessly abstract or less general than is possible. Law rarely can affect everyone identically, because people benefit or suffer from its burdens to different degrees. Even the roads we all use specially aid frequent drivers and burden disproportionately those whose property is taken by eminent domain. To project a ground for actual agreement we must consider these differences; they are best considered when we express and observe them tangibly. We will not observe concretely, however, if government is too remote, as it will be if left to executives alone—hence the virtue, low but solid, of representative assemblies that help law stay limited by keeping it realistic.

Why, then, are responsible legislatures insufficient to produce responsible government? The standard argument is that because we apply laws individually, legislatures that act as executives will unjustly distort laws' generality. The line between arbitrary and reasonable action would be blurred. This argument is important, but it considers execution as administration and does not look to what is desirable in executive action per se. Executive action is necessary and can be responsible because its constant overstepping enables a community to meet threats and seize opportunities that otherwise would overpower it. Legislatures alone cannot meet terrorist threats or double the size of countries through Louisiana Purchases. The continual reshaping by executives also enables a community to assimilate concerns that would be pushed aside in ordinary representative politics. Our greater executives see before others do the need to create friendships, prepare for battle, and admit new talent, because they see matters in an enterprising light. Responsible executive energy and enterprise are useful in a world that does not stand still even when we mean government to be limited. They also are desirable because they allow the country to express the farther reaches of responsibility and to domesticate spirited pride by giving it a central political outlet.[41]

The successful executive, however, still would be too dominant were he not opposed by others of his own type. Legislatures and legislators are neither swift nor bold enough to restrict executive action properly. In our domestic federalism, enterprising governors and ambitious agency heads limit presidents. More fundamentally, we limit political executives through the vast areas we still reserve to the responsibility of private entrepreneurs and by the almost incredible distance our politics takes from controlling speech and religion. Within speech and religion we largely trust tolerance rather than censorship to restrict possible excess. Tolerance permits the rise of doctrines that, and doctrinaires who, compete and countervail. Whatever the competition, moreover, the American executive is, as we have said, by and large trained to take his bearings from liberal government's ordinary concerns. Crusades against illiteracy, wars on crime, and missions to save and promote democracy characterize our successful political leaders. Their reshaping, redefining, and reformulating remain responsibly directed to securing responsible freedom for others (and themselves) because they occur within the ambit of political competition and opinion that defends the equal protection of practical popular rights. It is just this protection that our founders created our institutions to serve.

It also is good that some in Congress act more as enterprising executives than as ordinary or even extraordinary compromisers. The legislature will be too weak unless some try to make it a vehicle for their own hopes. It also is useful that so many in the executive conduct themselves bureaucratically, with responsibilities seen as special elements within legislatively dominated activities. They regulate, adjust, ameliorate, enforce, and execute only within the compromises that enable their practices to be organized and funded. Unless this usually happened, legislative compromise would seldom be successful and the executive would become too contentious for the legislature to bear. Yet, were everyone in the executive branch to conduct himself this way we would not have responsible executive energy where it is necessary. Lasting free government is attained through a subtle mixture and expression of responsible enterprise and compromise.

Conclusion

I am arguing that responsibility is the standpoint from which effective government is (and should be) conducted in liberal democracies. Government's purpose is to secure the individual characteristics by which we can execute our equal liberty successfully, now and in the future. Not fearful accountability but effectively taking charge of more and more (and accounting to oneself and others for actually getting the job done) is the heart of responsibility as a virtue.

Responsible action is not automatic. As is true of all virtues, it requires training and proper conditions. It is challenged especially by narrow or lazy self-interest that forgets the conditions for future satisfaction. Yet, it is consistent with self-interest when self-interest extends itself. As the disposition that organizes skills and talents so that they can be effective, moreover, responsibility is not merely another skill or talent. Also, the knowledge that guides it is not itself an art or technique. Rather, it is practical or political, in the ways I have described. The two characteristic directions of responsibility are enterprise and compromise, modes of acting that fit together with ways of thinking politically. Enterprise is at home in the projecting and reaching out to the new that is characteristic of responsible executives. Compromise is at home in the organizing of what already is present into common interests that is characteristic of responsible legislators. Such actions take place within the familiar horizon of the satisfaction of desire and protection of rights that is enforced constitutionally or through statute. Both compromise and enterprise are allied to other modern virtues, to tolerance and being nice or "kind," and to industry and responsibility itself as effectively doing one's job. Either can degenerate—compromise, from responsible or just compromise to the mere balancing of narrow interests; enterprise, from responsible or magnanimous enterprise to extreme adventurism or worse. Not only education but also the clash of legislators or executives is needed to keep each in check and on his toes. This clash is similar to the spirit and limits of economic competition, and, accordingly, it does not occur, or occur well, without some explicit attention.

In the next chapter, I illustrate and develop these arguments by discussing foreign affairs, the emblematic instance of countries acting as a whole. I choose this because it best illustrates executive responsibility. I will touch on the connection between responsibility and domestic policy when I discuss professional life and biotechnology.

NOTES

1. This purpose is evident from the Declaration of Independence.

2. See John Locke, *Second Treatise of Government*, VII, 87, and Thomas Hobbes, *Leviathan,* chaps. 6, 10, 13, and 14.

3. For related but not identical reflections cf. Jacob Klein, "On the Nature of Nature," in his *Lectures and Essays*, edited by Robert B. Williamson and Elliott Zuckerman (Annapolis, Md.: St. John's College Press, 1985).

4. This view of natural authority could, of course, be challenged. Perhaps only communities are naturally authoritative, not individuals (consider Aristotle's discussion in Book I of the *Politics*). Perhaps some natural characteristics cover all their members but cover them unequally, as reason covers all humans who nonetheless are unequally rational. The common understanding of what nature means, that is to say, does not require liberal individualism. Indeed, substantive differences here are at the core of variations among political philosophers. For thinkers obviously have different views of what we truly mean by spontaneity and causality, of the various possibilities for universality and generality, and of what the natural things are concretely. Working out these conceptual differences belongs to the overall conceptual and historical task of political thought.

5. See Hobbes, *Leviathan*, chaps. 6, 12, 13, 14, and 21.

6. John Locke, *Essay Concerning Human Understanding*, II, 20. I discuss this question more fully in the closing chapter.

7. The academic literature on freedom is vast. A recent discussion of its meaning for liberal democracy is Henry Richardson, *Democratic Autonomy* (Oxford: Oxford University Press, 2002).

8. When we consider control and constraint we always implicitly have some such substance, some instances, in mind although we often bypass their nature analytically.

9. Consider John Locke, *Essay Concerning Human Understanding*, II, 21.

10. Consider the close of Leo Strauss's discussion of Locke in *Natural Right and History* (Chicago: University of Chicago Press, 1953).

11. The complexity of the connection between rights and freedoms or liberties sometimes causes us to speak of them identically. Both Locke and the Declaration of Independence speak of a right to liberty, however, so they are not always equivalent. When we do not use rights and liberty equivalently, we may understand the right to liberty as shorthand for "enjoy the fruits of one's liberty," or as referring to particular liberties, say, political liberty. More broadly, we may differentiate rights and liberties as follows: the right to liberty is the authority to use, direct, or enjoy one's own (natural) self-movement and lack of constraint as opposed to someone else's using it. If someone else uses or directs one's natural

liberty, of course, the distinction between the right to one's freedom and freedom simply seems practically irrelevant.

We see similar equivocation when we speak of equal opportunities, which we sometimes equate with equal rights. An opportunity is not an authority, however, so rights and opportunities are not strictly identical. Opportunity and chance do not carry the same weight as right. When equal opportunity is used identically to equal right, it refers to goods as objects of rightful equal access for pursuit, holding, or choosing (rather than to goods as what we would amass or be given in substantively equal amounts however responsible or energetic our pursuit). For goods to be pursued as equal opportunities we may require external equal conditions (markets, some degree of education, voting), some of which are the same as and some of which go beyond what we need if our equal authority is equally to begin to activate its responsibility and equally to possess (e.g., to possess legally and as its own) these (potentially unequal) results. It is sometimes more and sometimes less important practically to insist on these distinctions and on recognizing the different phenomena that underlie them.

12. Consider Locke's discussion of the suspension of desire in the *Essay*, II, 21.

13. Speaking generally, the characteristics that any form of government strives to produce and establish are visible in those who govern and in the way they govern.

14. This view is a significant part of the political science literature from at least the 1930s to the 1960s; the problem is evident as well in the work of Woodrow Wilson and in activity from the New Deal through the Eisenhower administration that sought to establish and defend a professional civil service and the kind of administrative staffs for presidents and cabinet officers that we have come to take for granted. Because bureaucracy (and administrative staff) was considered necessary for modern government, it had to be perfected or even established at the same time one tried to show that it could be responsible. For various discussions of these issues see, among others, Woodrow Wilson, "The Study of Administration," *Political Science Quarterly* 2 (June 1887): 197–222; Arthur A. Maass and Laurence I. Radway, "Gauging Administrative Responsibility," *Public Administration Review* 9 (Summer 1949): 182–92; and J. Roland Pennock, "Responsiveness, Responsibility and Majority Rule," *American Political Science Review* 46 (September 1952): 790–807.

15. Carl Joachim Friedrich and Taylor Cole, *Responsible Bureaucracy* (Cambridge, Mass.: Harvard University Press, 1932), 28. Friedrich, later to become president of the American Political Science Association, is, according to the book's preface, the primary author of the chapter from which this passage comes.

16. Austin Ranney, *The Doctrine of Responsible Party Government* (Urbana: University of Illinois Press, 1962), 14. (The book originally was published in 1954,

and the dissertation from which it was adapted was completed in 1948.) For additional elements of these arguments, see many of the readings collected in Dwight Waldo, *Ideas and Issues in Public Administration* (New York: McGraw-Hill, 1953). For the basic argument about political parties see, in addition to Ranney, the Committee on Political Parties of the American Political Science Association's report "Toward a More Responsible Two-Party System," Supplement to *American Political Science Review* 44 (September 1950).

17. Consider here *Federalist* 49 and chap. 5 below.

18. Consider *Federalist* 63.

19. I discuss enterprise and compromise more fully below.

20. Also, of course, it is usually difficult to separate one representative's contribution from another's.

21. For further discussion in this vein of American constitutionalism and of *The Federalist,* see, among other works, David Epstein, *The Political Theory of the Federalist* (Chicago: University of Chicago Press, 1984); Charles R. Kesler, ed., *Saving the Revolution* (New York: Free Press, 1987); James W. Muller, ed., *The Revival of Constitutionalism* (Lincoln: University of Nebraska Press, 1988); Harvey C. Mansfield, Jr., *Taming the Prince* (New York: Free Press, 1987); Harvey C. Mansfield, Jr., *America's Constitutional Soul* (Baltimore, Md: Johns Hopkins University Press, 1991); and several essays, including Charles R. Kesler, "Responsibility in *The Federalist,*" in *Educating the Prince,* ed. Mark Blitz and William Kristol (Lanham, Md.: Rowman and Littlefield, 2000).

22. For further consideration of these issues one should examine *The Federalist* and Locke's *Second Treatise.* I have discussed these questions further in an unpublished paper, "Self-Interest and Responsibility."

23. In this sense government officials are responsible for the long-term effectiveness of free government itself, inasmuch as in the last analysis responsible individuals are accountable to themselves for the possibility of their continued effectiveness.

24. The issues of bureaucratic responsibility offer especially interesting links and contrasts to the problems of professional responsibility that I will discuss in the fourth and fifth chapters.

25. The view that bureaucratic and political responsibility differ in kind would follow from the strict separation of politics and administration, a division that strikes many people as plausible at first glance. This separation often is associated with the work of Frank Goodnow. See Frank J. Goodnow, *Politics and Administration* (New York: Macmillan, 1900).

26. The classic discussion of bureaucracy occurs in the writings of Max Weber. A useful selection of Weber's writings has been translated by H. H. Gerth and C. Wright Mills: *From Max Weber* (Oxford: Oxford University Press, 1958).

The material on bureaucracy can be found on pp. 196–244, with Weber's view of the characteristics of bureaucracy (roughly, what I am calling here the picture-book portrayal) to be found on pp. 196–98.

27. A fine discussion of contemporary American bureaucracies can be found in James Q. Wilson, *Bureaucracy* (New York: Basic Books, 1989). For schools, consider, among others, Chester E. Finn, Jr., *We Must Take Charge* (New York: Free Press, 1991); J. S. Coleman, T. Hoffer, and S. Kilgore, *High School Achievement* (New York: Basic Books, 1982); Peter W. Cookson, Jr., *School Choice* (New Haven, Conn.: Yale University Press, 1994); S. C. Purkey and M. S. Smith, "Effective Schools: A Review," *Elementary School Journal* 83 (1983): 427–52; many works by Diane Ravitch, including *Left Back* (New York: Simon and Schuster, 2000); and ongoing assessments of education by the Heritage Foundation and other public policy research organizations.

28. See Dinesh D'Souza, *Ronald Reagan* (New York: Free Press, 1997); Kiron Skinner, Annelise Anderson, and Martin Anderson, eds., *Ronald Reagan, A Life in Letters* (New York: Free Press, 2003); and Margaret Thatcher, *Statecraft* (New York: HarperCollins, 2002).

29. Consider here the categories of bureaucratic types that Wilson provides on pp. 158–71 of *Bureaucracy*.

30. See *Los Angeles Times,* January 27, 2004, A1. The joint congressional and September 11 commission reports talk generally about agencies and sometimes about their heads and other senior officials. But there is little about what actual working officials should have done concretely at specific junctures with the resources at hand.

31. Consider Wilson, passim, as well as James Q. Wilson, *Varieties of Police Behavior* (Cambridge, Mass.: Harvard University Press, 1983.)

32. Describing the California budget crisis in the summer of 2003, Senator John Vasconcellos, a Democrat who was the state's longest-serving legislator, said: "A third of the folks have been here for six months and they walk into a $38 billion hole. There is no mentoring. No seasoning. No history. No loyalty. This is an awesome responsibility. Not just a trite piece of work. You really have to understand what's going on." Willie Brown, former speaker of the Assembly, claimed that an important element of the problem came from "the absence of what I believe is the key ingredient in the legislative process: personal friendships." *Los Angeles Times,* July 29, 2003, A18.

33. What such a code might properly require—that a government scientist not distort his results because a superior asks him to, for example—is not different from what effective service in a regime of varied offices and powers requires. If it is different, by what argument could one show that it is just that the professional should prevail over the political? Neither immediate accountability nor extrapolitical

professional accountability but, rather, political responsibility, should be the guide. To the degree that discussions of bureaucratic responsibility—such as the then well known debate nearly two-thirds of a century ago between Herman Finer and Carl Friedrich—are seen primarily as debates between unmediated accountability to popular interests and accountability to professional norms, the issue is miscast. See Carl J. Friedrich, "Responsibility and Policy Formation," *Public Policy: 1940,* ed. Carl J. Friedrich and Edward S. Mason (Cambridge, Mass.: Harvard University Press, 1940); and Herman Finer, "Administrative Responsibility in Democratic Government," *Public Administration Review* 1 (1941). Long excerpts from both articles can be found in Alan A. Altshuler and Norman C. Thomas, eds. *The Politics of the Federal Bureaucracy,* 2nd ed. (New York: Harper and Row, 1977).

34. Consider here Havel's view, and the difference between Churchill, with his great abilities and complex tasks in the Second World War and vast perspective before it, and other "responsible" British officials.

35. Consider Richardson's discussion of practical knowledge in *Democratic Autonomy.*

36. On the executive one might consider further Peter Drucker, *The Effective Executive* (New York: Harper and Row, 1967); Carnes Lord, *The Modern Prince* (New Haven, Conn.: Yale University Press, 2003); and Mansfield, *Taming the Prince.*

37. On the Cold War consider John Lewis Gaddis, *We Now Know* (New York: Oxford University Press, 1997). I develop examples from foreign policy at length in the next chapter.

38. We will not all agree that all these actions are good, though most will admire them in some way. Enterprising responsibility is a basic way our institutions work when they are successful, but it does not guarantee good outcomes—outcomes that secure responsible character. Nothing can guarantee them, although to help bring them about the clash of entrepreneurs, and compromise, are necessary.

39. The classic formulation is Hobbes's state of nature.

40. On the legislator's skill consider Robert Dallek, *Flawed Giant: Lyndon Johnson and His Times* (New York: Oxford University Press, 1998); and William Bulger, *While the Music Lasts* (New York: Houghton Mifflin, 1996).

41. Consider Hamilton's discussion of the executive in *Federalist* 67.

3

RESPONSIBILITY AND FOREIGN AFFAIRS

What should be the purpose of our foreign policies? Why might someone spend time away from private interests or domestic politics to become engaged in them? What prevents such engagement from becoming a field for imperial ambition, as it has been historically from the Athenian Alcibiades to contemporary tyrants? How can our multiple agencies and divided government ever produce policy that is sensible and coherent?

In one way or another, the responses to these questions involve the way we protect equal liberty or equal rights. Following my theme, I intend to organize my discussion around responsibility. Responsibility is, of course, not the only phenomenon worth exploring here, but properly understood it is especially significant because it is central in the actual exercise of our rights. It enables us to look beyond liberties statically described to our form of government actively in motion. Indeed, the expression and clash of responsibilities is a—perhaps the—safeguard of liberty.

Much of this chapter tries to display how this clash works politically. The remainder develops the argument that our foreign policies should foster responsible freedom, our own and to a lesser extent others'. Seeing things as a responsible man sees them, moreover, should be the standard for our judgments and involvement. As before, my theoretical point will be that a link exists between the virtues that American life tries to enhance in its citizens and the virtues that we require to make our institutions function well. End and form work together, and the virtue of responsibility is a central element in both. This is as true of foreign as of domestic matters.

REALISM AND IDEALISM

It may seem obvious that our foreign policies should promote responsibility. Who would be mad enough to say they should foster the opposite? Blithe disregard, reckless abandon, feckless frittering away of power and substance—these are platform planks that none could knowingly love. Yet, much we do abroad is not very different from what would result were irresponsibility our conscious guide. Policies shaped by economic interest alone, for example, or by national interest otherwise narrowly construed, treat others' religion, hopes for liberal freedom, and possible democratic institutions as odd irritants to be dismissed, ignored, or wished away. People who themselves would not yield an ounce of liberty for a pound of flesh repeatedly act as if others will. The endless surprise when economic ties and mutual advantage do not always lead others to gaze lovingly when Americans wander into sight is an example of this mistake. A shock to such "realism" has been a recurring feature of our Mideast affairs, from Iran to Afghanistan to Iraq.

Iran, of course, took its hostages during the administration of our most famously moralistic president since Woodrow Wilson. Jimmy Carter's moralism, and moralism generally, lead us to wield power with guilt and therefore poorly, to cede our authority to international bodies or make nervous excuses when we do not, and to overlook our interests. No serious or responsible politician should entertain legalistic or "disinterested" obedience to the Kyoto Accords, the International Criminal Court, or their thousand cousins of the past (such as the Law of the Sea Conventions) or future.[1] A moralistic belief in internationalism, in fact, often is inseparable from the wish to divest ourselves of the responsibility that comes with our power, if not from that power itself.

Although realism and moralism lead to foolish disregard of facts and to inattention to power or an inability to use it, neither leads or has yet led us to wild adventurism. Their irresponsibility stems from the wishful thinking of hard or soft men, but it is not boldly reckless or tyrannical action. Perhaps liberals were honest when they treated President Reagan's Strategic Defense Initiative as the height of recklessness—made worse by its being poised against the "evil" empire. Perhaps they mean it when they fear President Bush's "axis of evil" will tempt him to extreme measures. I myself believe that neither of these charges was intended seriously. I doubt that those who opposed attacking Iraq really believed it to be recklessly wild (as opposed to something they themselves might not have done) or that anyone but a deterrent theologian actually believes the common sense of strategic defense to be outlandishly extreme and not merely uncomfortably new and expensive. I doubt as well that liberals and conservatives who opposed intervention in Bosnia, Haiti, or even Somalia truly believed it to be boundlessly excessive and not just imprudent. The overstatement in all these cases is more political than genuine.

I emphasize these points because the absence of wild adventure or extremism even in what some consider our most excessive foreign policies teaches us something about responsibility. The classic forms of irresponsible adventurism are present in tyrants' wishes to shatter and dominate or in proud men's hopes to make themselves imperial gods or figures of noble renown. We think of Alexander conquering the Persians, of Alcibiades fighting for Sparta against his Athenian homeland, of Napoleon's conquest of Europe, of the murderous lives of Stalin and Hitler.

We should not underestimate the significance of America's domestic freedom from such characters. At the country's beginning it could hardly be taken for granted. It was a staple of political rhetoric to claim that Hamilton, Burr, or Jefferson wished to be another Bonaparte.[2] As it turned out, however, our foreign (and domestic) affairs began to operate within the horizon of and for the protection of equal rights. The design of the founders forced political ambition and activity in the milder direction in fact that they had intended in principle. It is a political blessing that here the tall trees always are based in the egalitarian forest.

We nonetheless need something of the spirit of noble pride if we are to meet the threat of tyrannical figures from abroad. The Roosevelts and Douglas MacArthur, not to mention Washington and Lincoln, are necessary (or rise to the fore) in our direst circumstances or when our way of life is founded and secured. One of the remarkable features of American statesmanship is how we successfully redirect outstanding political capacity to liberal democratic ends without so stunting this capacity that we inevitably find it shriveled when we wish to see it bloom.[3] Whatever the irresponsibility of our actions, fostering tyranny is infrequently among them.

The fact that responsibility is both end and means in our regime helps to explain what substitutes democratically for political or imperial excess, provides a standpoint that overcomes the mistaken extremes of realism and idealism, and explains more ordinary—if still exceptional—attention to foreign affairs. Responsible action pursued by those who enjoy naturally equal rights leads to clashes of officials and candidates that limit excess while providing a controlled direction for spirited pride. At the same time, responsibility is not blindly or shortsightedly selfish, because responsibility is a virtue. Nor is it foolishly idealistic, because it is rooted in intelligent self-interest. As a virtue, responsibility belongs to a more commonsensical perspective than does "morality" as we discuss it under Kant's influence, or the narrowness of a self-interest that modern philosophers isolate from the natural search for happiness.

COHERENCE IN FOREIGN AFFAIRS

One might argue that clashing responsibilities is not as desirable as I am making it seem. Does it not often lead to political gridlock or, worse, to confusion and incoherence? In foreign policy in particular, one might suggest that the result of our struggles is that we fail to complete important jobs, leaving cacophony to replace the apparently steadier course of realism or moralism. I will examine this objection (and show responsibility at work) by developing the implications of specific actions that I was able to observe as they were occurring.

In June 1985, the Senate voted to repeal the so-called Clark Amendment of 1974, which, in effect, had prohibited our government from aiding rebels in the African country of Angola. The Reagan administration had not requested the repeal, there had been no committee testimony about it, and debate had been confined to ten minutes on the Senate floor. The House did not discuss the issue at all, accepting the Senate's action in a conference report the substance of which was determined by negotiations left almost exclusively to staff.

Throughout 1985, to take a second example, attempts were made to derail President Reagan's decision that international communications satellites separate from the Intelsat system were in the national interest. The effect of the president's decision was to permit competition with Intelsat's global monopoly. Intelsat hired lobbyists to invent strategies to overturn or neuter the policy and to pursue these strategies with all the vigor, sincerity, and casuistry that they could muster. Many were chosen because of political or personal friendship with those they were lobbying, or their staffs. Most were attorneys, who nonetheless approached their work in a manner indistinguishable from those without the protection and pretense of practicing law.

On the other side were the private firms that wished to launch the new satellites, the Federal Communications Commission, the Commerce Department's National Telecommunications Information Administration, and the State Department's Bureau of International Telecommunications. Their unity had resulted in the president's decision in the first place. It was hard won and often in danger of self-destruction. At least two of the agencies could barely conceal their contempt for each other, and one was a congressional invention for which no administration had ever asked. Indeed, the Bureau of International Telecommunications no longer exists.

All these groups directed their attention to four foreign affairs and four more commerce committees in the Senate and House, seeking or warding off hearings and legislation by reminding committees of their supposed jurisdictional responsibilities and producing suggestions to implement those interests. They offered and countered technical arguments about transmission capabilities, demographic trends, market capabilities, and the like. They invoked multilateral organizations (the International Telecommunications Union), bilateral relations, and the rhetoric of competition and privatization. They stimulated and calmed partisan passions, maneuvered, dissembled, and pressured. A vague but unmistakable odor of vanity, greed, and ambition enveloped the proceedings. In fact, the contested issues were early versions of today's raging debates about both the scope of communications ownership and American cultural imperialism.

As a third example, let us consider again the same conference discussions between the House and the Senate that repealed the Clark Amendment, but focus now on the heated debate that occurred about "Cocom," a group composed of representatives from certain countries and several agencies of the U.S. government that decided what products contained technologies too sensitive to be exported to what we then called the Eastern Bloc. The conference debate centered on the relative responsibility of the Defense Department, known to want severe export restrictions, and the State Department, thought to have more moderate views, though less moderate than those of the sales-driven Commerce Department. Arguments about technology sales and predictable disputes between State and Defense remain features of today's daily politics. The disputes about and within Cocom had been media events during President Reagan's first term, featuring as they did the mixture of money, national security, and gossip about the powerful, dear to contemporary writers and readers. A member of the House of Representatives was forcing the issue and promoting the State Department view, largely, as best anyone could tell, because of personal dislike for a key member of the Defense Department. Some Senate staff made defense of the executive's position a central goal of the entire conference proceedings, buttressed by the official himself but not by the executive branch as a whole, the support of which was nominal. The compromise reached on Cocom favored the Defense Department's position but at some expense to the administration's position on the satellite issue. Staff could not allow the legislator who lost on Cocom to be defeated visibly on a second matter crucial to him.

As a final example, also echoed today, years of American concern about our treatment in the United Nations came to a head in the 1985 congressional appropriations and authorization process. Amendments in earlier years that restricted funding to the United Nations because of its disgraceful behavior toward Israel were now enhanced by still more amendments inspired by further disgraces, fears of spying under UN cover, and gross overspending. These amendments were largely the creatures of junior legislators and their staffs, often working with think tanks like the Heritage Foundation. The executive branch had asked for none of the amendments, although President Reagan's unhappiness with the UN was well known. Some amendments were quietly supported by the intelligence agencies, however, and the committees that oversee them. The State Department fought them all, those supported by the intelligence community more vigorously than others. The State Department's own fiscal crisis, however—its need to support its basic operations and at the same time to fund massive new physical security measures for its embassies abroad—enabled it to see the utility of freeing extra funds for its own purposes. Its ardor for the fight to protect the UN therefore was dampened. Various outside groups fought more vigorously, and members of the UN high command, including the secretary general, pleaded directly with key legislators. They found surprisingly little congressional support. The traditional legislative allies of the United Nations understood the difficulty of their cause. More significantly, they very much desired successful legislation and did not want authorization and appropriations bills stalled. The result was an important change in our financial relations with the United Nations that the Reagan administration had not organized and the congressional leadership had not instigated.

The same authorization process from which I have drawn these four examples also permitted the continued operation abroad of hundreds of embassies, consulates, and cultural centers. It supported thousands of hours of radio broadcasting, millions of dollars of academic scholarships, and countless trips, visits, conferences, and negotiations. It authorized salaries for myriads of diplomats, bureaucrats, clerks, and political officials ensconced in the State Department, the Agency for International Development, and the United States Information Agency (which during the Clinton administration was dismembered, with most parts relocated to State, in still another process that the executive branch had not originally begun). It permitted land to be rented, buildings to be built, contracts to be let, and all of this to be investigated, audited, evaluated, and studied. Remarkably, however, the executive branch conducted with a free hand the vast majority of these broadcasts, scholarships, negotiations, audits, discussions, and diplomatic missions. Although previously legislated standards guided this activity and the new authorizing bill implicitly or explicitly reaf-firmed these codes, Congress exercised little practical oversight. In the great bulk of detailed business, the executive administered, and still administers, largely unchecked. This leeway is remarkable even today in places such as Iraq and Afghanistan, directly within the public glare.

From such examples, readily multiplied, one might conclude that American government is too fragmented to be effective, that its clash-ing centers of responsibility ordinarily lead to situations in which lit-tle good is achieved. Yet, these very examples contain instances of far-reaching activity that was accomplished quickly, easily, silently, and largely unopposed. Perhaps, then, the dangerous issue is not ineffec-tiveness but incoherence. Over the long term, however, things seem much less incoherent than they do at any moment. The repeal of the Clark Amendment fit with the Reagan administration's anticommu-nist policy in southern Africa, the limits on UN spending became part of an American effort that still exists simultaneously to rational-ize the United Nations and diminish its significance, and the debates we continue to have about international telecommunications are nor-mal expressions of financial competition amid changing technology, well on this side of the boundaries of debilitating confusion.

When we consider larger issues we also should doubt the view that incoherence and ineffectiveness are rampant. President Reagan was able to reorient strategic thinking and to achieve massive budget outlays for his Strategic Defense Initiative with surprisingly little staff discussion, bureaucratic competition, or congressional opposition. Some hurdles existed then, and they continue to exist to the current versions of strategic defense. Do these hurdles display incoherence and fecklessness or, rather, sober caution in the face of remarkable ex-ecutive energy? President Bush is spending huge amounts in Iraq with disproportionately little oversight and has begun to transform the structure and doctrines of the American military against real but, given the scope of the reform, unremarkable opposition. Does this not display effectiveness rather than the opposite? Do the various mil-itary, domestic, and judicial measures to fight terrorism, with the many-sided debates and judgments that shape these actions, show in-coherence or, rather, an effective effort to face terrorism while not re-stricting liberty irresponsibly?

THE POLICY ATMOSPHERE

I conclude from these examples and others that our political struggles in foreign affairs result in more effective coherence than we sometimes think. The first reason is the essentially political conduct that we have been discussing, in which legislative compromise, executive enterprise, bureaucratic effectiveness, and more narrow self-interest work together to produce sometimes limited and sometimes bold results, all open to continual readjustment. The second reason is that this conduct occurs within the horizon of the responsible execution of individual rights and the restricted goals and constitutional forms that direct and organize this conduct.[4]

These forms and restrictions do not work automatically. They require both education and the press of responsible action as it pushes beyond the tasks or narrow interests that initiate it. In politics, a position in government—in Congress, say, or even merely as a voter—makes you a force to be reckoned with and sets the direction of your acts and others' efforts to persuade and cajole you. This is why it is so foolish to ignore actual formal assignments and rush to explain politics mostly in terms of behavior (or even character) abstracted from position. Of course, how far and with how much responsibility you actually carry out your tasks is less determined. This fluidity is a condition for the political atmosphere of enterprise, compromise, and bureaucratic action, and is necessary if responsibility is to be connected to freedom and not become a word for routinized or slavish obedience.

Let me develop this point still further. Within a political situation, one begins by recognizing what is given. If many agencies are engaged in an issue, one deals with them; if Congress is involved, one deals with it. One normally neither wishes nor needs more institutions and officials involved than have involved themselves already. But restricting agencies and Congress is difficult, for if an issue at all touches one's legal or bureaucratic competence, one can engage it. The enormous number of military, intelligence, foreign affairs, and domestic agencies concerned with some aspect of security against terror is striking. The same complexity is evident also in less pressing foreign matters.

Possibilities for involvement are not unbounded, and within the executive they come to a head with the president. Nonetheless, varied involvement in issues cannot easily be controlled. Moreover, inciting congressional committees or executive agencies to action often is a strategy for getting one's own way. Within any agency, moreover, bureaucrats constantly bring their disputes to a higher level or threaten to do so. Immediate supervisors try to limit this practice, but distant supervisors try to permit it. If someone already has control, he does not wish to involve others; restricting the competition, thereby attaining policy or administrative monopoly, is everyone's usual desire and on many small issues the usual outcome. But no official believes he controls enough. Everyone, therefore, both wants and does not want strict hierarchy, limited involvement, and full coordination.

This ambiguity and fluidity make it difficult for responsibility to become overweening pride or great or petty tyranny. During President Reagan's first term, for example, funding and direction of our foreign aid program were controlled by the White House together with the relevant appropriations subcommittees. The House and Senate authorizing committees were unable to pass foreign aid and security assistance bills. At the beginning of Reagan's second term the authorizing committees, under the new leadership of Senator Lugar and Congressman Fascell, were determined to pass legislation and regain some control. The administration, however, had become comfortable dealing only with the appropriations committees. Foreign aid is contentious and is disliked by many citizens. Why give unpopular programs extra chances to be attacked? The administration therefore was cool to the authorizers' efforts. Nonetheless, once the authorizing committees made clear that they were likely to succeed—that, indeed, they would pass several amendments disapproved by the administration if they were ignored—the administration, which relied on the committees for other support, was forced to work and compromise with them. The small circle that for years controlled foreign aid had been opened.

RESPONSIBILITY AND THE CONDUCT OF FOREIGN AFFAIRS

I am arguing that the incoherence and ineffectiveness that might result from this process in fact do not, perhaps surprisingly. One believes that with so many involved in so many different issues, spectacular confusion would result. Yet we have seen that nearly single-minded control and action sometimes occur, and that what seems episodic often fits into a sensible frame. The truth is that wandering as the course of affairs sometimes may appear, both the general direction and the specific goals of American foreign policy have been quite clear since the Second World War. One reason for such coherence and effectiveness is that legislative compromise produces the kinds of measures I have been discussing. It considers and adjusts interests in light of a common ground the importance of which is freshly but obviously visible; in the case of the Homeland Security Bill, for example, what is visible is the new need for coordination that those who deal with immigration, transportation, and education now face. A second reason is the assertion of executive responsibility that looks far ahead to the country's future. It sees matters such as armed intervention abroad and domestic police powers in a new light. In the case of terrorism, what some had thought to be essential elements of "democracy"— empty self-determination rather than genuine self-government abroad and the legitimacy of every domestic assertion of extreme rights far removed from natural liberty—are no longer widely seen to be central or even proper. What comes to the fore is a better grasp of the requirements, conditions, and responsibilities of liberal democracy, for ourselves and others. Both coherence and self-limitation in policy arise from responsibly prosecuting tasks that must take the long view.

RESPONSIBLE DIRECTIONS FOR FOREIGN POLICY

The question I wish to develop now is what responsibility—both as a goal to seek and as a standpoint from which to judge—indicates about guiding foreign affairs. I will mention six areas, three of them concerning ways and means, and three that are more immediately substantive.

First is to remind ourselves again of what is visible in the discussions I just concluded: the significant place of Congress and not only the executive in foreign affairs. The Constitution indicates preeminence for the president as commander in chief, but this preeminence stands within overall shared responsibility for budgets and treaties.[5] Such shared responsibility is nothing new. Serious discussions in the Washington and Adams administrations of policy toward France and Great Britain, and of raising an army and navy, were hardly confined to the executive alone. They were central also to the legislative debates, public opinion, and electoral politics of the day. Jefferson's Louisiana Purchase was a bold assertion of executive enterprise, but it could not have been assimilated without legislative compromise and support. Responsible legislators to this day must work with the executive to secure effective programs and useful appropriations. They are the ones who must derail inappropriate treaties and other potential mistakes. They also often take larger steps, because the character and views that lead them to perform sometimes thankless public tasks also drive them to examine territory the executive has not yet occupied. The Nunn-Lugar Act, which seeks to limit nuclear proliferation effectively, is a good example from recent years. Congressional responsibility, properly understood, checks executive pretension, works together with the executive to meet necessities, and sometimes presses forward where the president himself has not taken the lead. The tendency to defer to the executive in the battle against terrorism is understandable and to a degree desirable but harmful when it becomes excessive.

Second (as I suggested earlier) is to be cautious of internationalism. By internationalism I mean ceding authority to international bodies as opposed to working with allies toward a common goal. To allow international courts and political entities serious authority is to restrict freedom, for to promote freedom practically is to promote the habit of its use: to encourage freedom is to support the growth and exercise of responsibility. To advance the exercise of responsibility, therefore, is to begin along a path that encourages all people to engage to some degree in public affairs and several to engage in it significantly. Increased internationalism, however, makes government ever more remote from citizens and restricts active attention. Officious bureaucrats elected by no one, or those who do not believe in free government in the first place, are the ones who make decisions. The spectacle of tyrants excluding the United States from international human rights bodies is appalling. The tendency of some European governments to decide that the citizens of other democracies should not be subject to these countries' own laws is disturbing.[6] Judicial control is promoted through international courts and other bodies whose norms and procedures are alien to our own. Legislative and bureaucratic activities are conducted at far removes from effective representation. Whatever gain internationalism brings in security is countered by a loss in self-government, not only ours but also that of other free countries. National governments are imperfect, but their imperfections are by and large worsened, not improved, by the remoteness of international regimes. In fact, the size, distance, unclear goals, and potential dominance of these groups is such that the difficulties I have mentioned would exist even were international bodies collections of perfectly republican governments, as of course they are not. Free governments must be composed of actively free citizens.

Third is responsible intervention in areas beyond our immediate interests. By responsible intervention I mean intervention measured carefully by our resources, the importance and urgency of the situation, others' need for self-reliance, and our own understanding of ourselves as standing for what is right. Responsibility obviously argues against feckless gestures and unbalanced use of resources. It also points away from a moralism that is disconnected from our own interests and that fails to see others' freedoms in the context of theirs. In its broader political meaning, however, it precludes mere calculation (because we connect interests to the exercise of equal rights) and excessive control (because we are concerned with others' self-government). Narrow self-interest alone will not induce us to take risks to help others attain their freedoms, even though these freedoms may help us in the long run.[7] To measure possible intervention responsibly, however, provides at best a standpoint for judgment, not a formula for application. It is a standpoint not terribly far from the considerations we have brought to bear throughout our history, and especially as our power has grown.

This leads to the question of the purposes of our policy, and here we should have in mind both "idealism" and "realism" considered responsibly. From the beginning of the United States our founders believed that regimes based on equal rights would dominate the future. The differences between, say, Jefferson and Adams in policies toward

Great Britain and France did not mean either thought that regimes based on standards other than those of equal rights are as just as those that are. No multiculturalism clouded their principled view. In my judgment it still is wise actively to promote equality of rights, religious tolerance, representative government, majority voting, and separation of powers. Responsibility in others should be our central goal in dealing with them. Such promotion—whether through prudent intervention, aggressive public diplomacy, or as the result of private action—has several advantages. It may seem to foster but actually restricts our potential arrogance, by reminding us that what is distinctive about us are principles that cover others as well as ourselves. It gives us a task and direction beyond self-interest narrowly conceived. Also, conducted intelligently, in the long run it promotes rather than restricts our security, because it expands our circle of friends. Our liberal principles, moreover, permit and encourage reasonable diversity in practices and beliefs not just among our own citizens but for the citizens of other countries who choose to be formed by these principles. Their spread is therefore not venally "imperialistic." It is true, nonetheless, that free government will color these practices in ways similar to the manner in which the responsible and tolerant character of liberally acquisitive citizens colors earlier notions of duty, obligation, and the public scope of faith.

I conclude with the points that strong defense and careful attention to economic interests also stem from the perspective of responsibility. For this standpoint is attentive to interest both in itself and as a necessary element of effective principle. Security is brought about by strength, not weakness or indifference, and security is a condition of freedom. John Adams once wrote that the peace missions he sent to France during his presidency "were the most disinterested and meritorious actions" of his life. "I reflect upon them," he continued, "with so much satisfaction that I desire no other inscription over my gravestone than: 'Here lies John Adams, who took upon himself the responsibility of the peace with France in the year 1800.'"[8] As Adams saw it, he could discharge this responsibility effectively only because at the same time we were beginning to build a navy strong enough to give others a reason to join us in our peaceful quest. Thoughtful American statesmen always have been aware that responsible statesmanship demands sufficient resources. To be effective and to continue to be effective, one cannot rely solely on goodwill or purity of intention, and surely not on wishful thinking.

NOTES

1. See Dinesh D'Souza, *Ronald Reagan* (New York: Free Press, 1997).

2. Consider, for example, material quoted or summarized in David McCullough, *John Adams* (New York: Simon and Schuster, 2001).

3. Consider John Keegan, *The Mask of Command* (New York: Penguin Books, 1988); Lord Charnwood, *Abraham Lincoln* (New York: Henry Holt, 1916); various biographies of Winston Churchill, such as Roy Jenkins, *Churchill* (New York: Farrar, Straus and Giroux, 2001); and Robert D. Kaplan, *Warrior Politics* (New York: Random House, 2001).

4. I will further discuss the grounds of natural rights in my final two chapters.

5. Consider Article I, Sections 7, 8, 9, and 10, and Article II, Sections 2 and 3 of the Constitution.

6. We should consider with concern the measures taken and threatened against Henry Kissinger and Ariel Sharon. Several recent works by Jeremy Rabkin are a good guide to this general issue. Representative are his testimony at the hearings on "International Justice," Committee on International Relations, U.S. House of Representatives, February 28, 2002; "The International Kangaroo Court," *Weekly Standard*, April 25, 2002; and "Human Rights Agenda versus National Sovereignty," which is part of Freedom House's Freedom in the World survey for 2000–2001. It is available on the Freedomhouse.org website. See also Jeremy Rabkin, *The Case for Sovereignty* (Washington, D.C.: AEI Press, 2004).

7. Self-interest, however, can sometimes go surprisingly far. Presumably, for example, it was the ground for much of France's help during our war for independence from Great Britain.

8. From McCullough, who refers to Ralph Waldo Brown, *The Presidency of John Adams* (Lawrence: University Press of Kansas, 1975), 174. Brown himself finds the quotation in Zoltan Haraszti, *John Adams and the Prophets of Progress* (New York: Grosset and Dunlap, 1964), 263.

4

LAW AND RESPONSIBILITY

Ituurn now to responsibility in our professions, especially as they serve a public purpose.[1] I will discuss law, the media, philanthropy, and liberal education. I intend to indicate how they exemplify responsibility and how it might guide them. Not only government but these practices affect public life and are areas of free, responsible action.

THE CURRENT CONTROVERSIES ABOUT LAW

I will begin to discuss law by reporting the current controversies about it. Many believe we have too many laws, too many lawsuits, and too many lawyers.[2] Walter Olson captures this concern with his phrase the "litigation explosion." One especially annoying cause of this explosion is grotesquely large tort awards. Asbestos, tobacco, and silicone-implant litigation make it evident that some lawyers irresponsibly inflate legitimate complaints or manufacture illegitimate ones.[3]

Many also believe that we have too little regularity in today's law, too little attention to the public interest, and too little punishment for miscreants. Philip Howard decries the death of common sense exemplified in the absurdity that replaces sensible handling of children's behavior in playgrounds and schools with adult litigiousness and political correctness. It seems at times as if our laws or at least our lawyers are the dreadful or ridiculous sophists of Plato's dialogues or Aristophanes's comedies.[4]

A bare recitation never can bring out vividly enough the thousand and one horrors that our legal system perpetrates. Examples are legion in the books I mentioned. But perhaps it is enough simply to imagine oneself caught in a legal vise and to linger in that vision, one's property made worthless by government's environmental intrusion, one's business bankrupted by liabilities one has only tenuously caused, one's ordinary reactions of praise and blame checked and distorted by lawsuits and their threat. In such a nightmare, pieties about the rule of law choke in one's throat.

These complaints typically are made by conservatives, although many "neutral" pundits, editorialists, and legislators sympathize with them and authorities recently have taken steps to redress them.[5] In any event, they are countered by attorneys who make opposing claims. They see defense of the weak and downtrodden where others see arbitrary excess. Trial lawyers believe that tort litigation, even with excessive awards, protects us from indifferent and complacent businessmen who poison the air, water, and our bodies. It enables us to hold unscrupulous financiers to account. It somewhat equalizes the wealthy and the poor. The true excess, in their view, is not in civil but in criminal law, with its unjust mandatory sentences, restrictions to judicial freedom, distortions of civil rights, and overall indifference to the plight of the poor.[6]

The conservative counter to this typically liberal view is that too few crimes are prosecuted to begin with and too many miscreants allowed to avoid their guilt. More broadly, attempting mechanically to balance conservative and liberal claims does not prove that the claims bear equal weight. Thoughtless evenhandedness leads us to evade choice and thus belongs to the very ethos of irresponsibility that is central to the law's current problems.

FORCE AND RESPONSIBILITY

I will organize my discussion of these issues and of law and responsibility generally around six points. The first concerns law's scope, because these accusations, balanced or not, make evident the peculiar range of the law. Law touches almost everything.[7] So, when we complain it can be hard to discern if we are worrying about law or about the subject with which some law deals. Concern about regulations that strangle the economy, for example, is as much a political as a legal issue. We do not lament only how laws are interpreted; we are concerned equally with whether the laws should be made at all. We cannot easily separate the rule of law (and the lawyers and judges who give it effect) from the politicians who make it. Richard Epstein constructs several simple rules to which he believes law should be reduced and from which it might sensibly flow. The rules would limit and clarify confusing and excessive litigation, but to adopt them would be a substantive political decision.

Law has not only wide range but remarkable strength. The helplessness in which we wallow while exploring each thread of the legal rope may lead us to overlook the cause of law's power—namely, its public force. One can throw aside a stupid article on harassment or eliminate with a satisfying click televised babble about my responsibility for your misdeeds, but legal proceedings that stem from such talk cannot be ignored without punishment. Some combination of lawyers' frightening power and their misuse of it is behind the thousands of jokes we tell about them and the contempt in which we hold or affect to hold them. Because of lawyers' public importance, their irresponsibility affects us more than does, say, businessmen's cheating.

My second point is that we should understand how directly American law and lawyers affect responsibility. Laws affect responsibility because of their substance—their impact on character and on the institutions that shape it. Law also affects responsibility because it is a profession that (may) embody it: lawyers and judges ought to be and usually are responsible, and we ask them as officers of the court to adhere to formal professional standards of responsibility.[8] In fact, many consider law to be the exemplary case of professions and professionalism, the example that beauticians, morticians, and political consultants imitate when they try to dignify their jobs or convince us that they are not all equally untrustworthy and unscrupulous. Finally, law affects responsibility because accountability is central in judging civil liability and criminal guilt. Indeed, several aspects of the issues we just outlined center on responsibility—tort liability and criminal accountability most obviously.

Law's affect on responsibility is not accidental, for our purpose in legislating is to enhance responsible character. Legal limits on action have this in view; this suggests that the burden generally is against laws that restrict freedom. Civil trials and even criminal punishment seek to enhance individual choice and the conditions of self-understanding that ground it. Justice in these cases is not equalizing in order to equalize or advantaging through special treatment. (Rather, it is redressing unearned advantage.) Such equalizing detracts from acting effectively on one's own and from the common conditions such action requires.[9] Similarly, affirmative action and other instances of unmerited special treatment are unjust, because the root of justice for us is to treat the responsible and free as equally responsible and free. Equality before the law is central to law's justice.

It is possible to depart accidentally but with good will from equal responsibility, because what it demands sometimes is subtle. The uncertainties of subtlety, however, can easily become the duplicities of sophistry. Consider economic issues. What precisely does consumer responsibility mean when products have hidden features or choice is limited? In principle a consumer can discover almost anything about a product, but at what cost? In principle any worker can decide that some proposed employment contract is too onerous, but with what options? One would think, for example, that known and advertised harms from tobacco and spilled hot coffee are in one category and hidden defects in automobiles and pharmaceuticals in another. So, although responsibility is biased toward allowing competition and toward notions of acceptable risk that do not stifle choice, this preference cannot dispose of all issues, and it sometimes demands substantive regulation.[10]

JUSTICE

I have stated that the justice we seek through law centers on responsibility. To see this clearly, we should discuss more carefully what justice means. This is my third topic.[11] Unlike modern virtues that differ from ancient ones because they are not connected to a specific good, modern justice is almost as broad as ancient justice[12] The difference lies more in what is thought actually to be just than in justice's scope.[13]

We use the term "justice" less than we think, as often calling something right (or wrong) as "just." To do what is right is to do what is proper, what fits. It is to give to someone what belongs to him. "This violin is back in the hands of its rightful owner." What belongs is not only a matter of property, however, for the violin should fit hands that play well. When I say that giving someone a picture he loves (say, because a friend owned it) is "the right thing to do," moreover, I wish to put it where it belongs not according to title or skill but by attachment and sentiment. When I agree that "it is not right to treat her that way" because "she's done nothing to deserve it," I give her what fits or belongs not because of ownership, skill, or passion but through recompense for action and effort. (In this way too a just verdict is the right verdict because it retributes a crime by punishing the guilty.) So, doing what is right is doing what is fitting (what belongs) in terms of owning (being one with), using best (making the most of by being together with), enjoying (attaching), or equating. To do what is right is in these various ways to do what fits.

We also as often say "(un)fair" as "(un)just." A "just result" after a dispute is "fair" to both parties. Someone fair does not take too much, give too little to others, or push them to the edge. She may even be very fair-minded—that is, give them what is right even if their claim could be questioned. It is "so unfair" (or, also "not right") that an inheritance goes to the wealthy selfish son, not the thoughtful, impoverished daughter. It is equally "unfair" when a tornado destroys her home, not his, even if both obtained their homes "fair and square," without cheating. What is fair also concerns what fits or belongs, proper distribution for the sake, or in the light, of proper connection.[14]

I should mention two other uses of "just." One is the seemingly trivial statement that an expression is *just* so—a person "just so impossible," a flower or picture arrangement "just right," or that the rain came "just in time." What is "just" here is to be precise or exact, with nothing left over or needing to be added; this use also is an instance of the just as what is proper and fitting, or, indeed, the just as the epitome of what is proper, perfect, and exemplary. The arrangement that is just right, moreover, the musician who begins to play at just the right moment, the students who line up in just the right order, or the coach who achieves just the right mix of players makes evident that the standpoint for what is just right can be a common and not only an individual enterprise.

One also can be too precise, of course; the precise can become the punctilious and overwhelm the fitting. Here, the just as the "righteous," our next use, shades into righteousness or self-righteousness. This occurs where one stays on a path (one is "correct") that deviates from its original purpose and forgets or ignores the other paths that might reach the end. The "right" way to do things tries to reach the goal, and to reach it in a certain manner. It fittingly puts together the pieces or steps. The way, however, can come to seem more important than the end. To be very proper is never to deviate from a code, practice, or rule (say, of etiquette) even when its source and point has been forgotten or, indeed, now is being contradicted. Even the (old) slang "righteous" means being made worthy by keeping the faith, being true to heroes and activities, being loyal.[15]

These examples ("just so," "righteous") enrich but do not change the root meaning of the just as what fits. The just may become a right or correct way that, as a way, as a rule or law, breaks free from actually accomplishing what is fitting or reaching its end. A punishment may be unjustly harsh in the circumstances or wrong and unfair when compared to similar cases; to stay with the legal way too closely is sometimes to be as officious as a bureaucrat. Yet to deviate from it is often to be arbitrary and unfair, for to be fair is often simply to give equal shares to equal owners rather than to give each what he can use best. The key point is that the just is the fitting or what belongs; as the right and fair, it can shade into the correct, narrow, and legal way, and the merely equal.

JUSTICE AND RESPONSIBILITY

The meaning of justice as fitting distribution (of benefits, burden, recompense, etc.) does not tell us automatically what counts as fair. It is easy to see that the better violin should go to the better violinist, but harder to decide whether the violinist should properly use his gifts to play, compose, or teach mathematics, and perhaps more difficult yet to decide how to adjudicate the different claims of property, skill, and affection. Perhaps with sufficient grasp of all that fits, together with a clear understanding of the conditions of responsibility, we might make more headway than we often believe.[16] This is not obvious, however. Nor does seeing what justice means make clear immediately what the scope should be of explicit attempts to secure justice through law and lawyers (rather than through private choice), our topic here. We must therefore examine these issues.

We begin by suggesting that in liberal democracies we orient what is legally right toward one leading kind of equal distribution: our explicit legal justice usually involves equal access to goods, to "opportunities."

Given our differences, however, in terms of what do we justly distribute equal access? The equality fittingly secured is our equal authoritative liberty, our equal right to choose how to accumulate and enjoy property, and our equal right to direct our lives. Legal limits on actions are intended to protect or enhance this equal freedom and the conditions we require to use it effectively, privately and in public. Such equal freedom permits possibly unequal results because of differences in effort, talent, and luck.[17] We do not intend substantive differences connected to unequal success to deflect this root equality. It might seem, however, that not only success but even the ability or permission to begin to enjoy some goods is unequally distributed. Untrammeled political speech, for example, which is a condition for securing equal rights, does not require enforceably equal access to writing for, rather than buying, the *New York Times*. Yet, the *Times* cannot prevent someone from issuing his own broadside or from writing for them simply because he is black or Catholic, although religions and clubs can define themselves in ways that restrict private access. (We differentiate between public accommodations and private groups.) Moreover, we do not require the *Times* to hire the illiterate. Our standard (with all the loosening consequent to modern substantive notions of equality) seems to be that we can use only relevant distinctions to differentiate people's effective equal access to institutions and opportunities, and that purely ascriptive qualities are not relevant.

We might think that the difference between permissible and proscribed distinctions is identical to the difference between native qualities and those assumed voluntarily. This is not so. Intelligence and athletic skill are only partially self-developed, yet they are reasonable grounds for differentiating some opportunities. Religion is (for us) a voluntary matter, yet it is not a reasonable ground for differentiating opportunities.

How, then, does our law see these discriminations and nondiscriminations consistently? Our equal freedom responsibly to acquire, produce, and enjoy property requires a point of view that encourages an acquisitive attitude, one open to a multitude of satisfactions. Many religions limit this reigning public perspective, so we choose through toleration to make religion a private matter. Although we select religion voluntarily, therefore, it is an illegitimate grounds for permissible legal discrimination, because all are equal politically. The other areas of acceptable public differentiation are, as we suggested, more directly attributable to the talent or skill required for the job to be done.

These distinctions are imperfect. They indicate, however, that the condition we use to judge legal justice is what fits the responsible individual. The equally rightful acquirer of property is not merely the episodic actor but the steady character who secures his success and advances from it effectively. It is for this character as well that we justify affirmative or substantive requirements, such as public education. Law's purpose is to help secure equal rights and the conditions that promote their responsible use. It is not to advance equal distribution of income or a defined set of satisfactions. The defects of our law are defects in terms of this purpose.

LEGAL COMPETITION

My fourth point is that attorneys and judges themselves belong to the competitive structure of American public life. Their job, their responsibility, is to be effective in pursuing justice within this clashing whole. This is true generally, not simply for adversarial trials. Judges, of course, are expected to be judicious. This means only that to do their work effectively they must be measured, because their work is the umpire's work of fair enforcement (even when new circumstances require novel applications of familiar law). What they enforce are laws the practical, political origin of which should be to encourage the maximum effect from free, responsible action.

Judges are constrained by the cases they take, by conditions of their appointment or election, and by superior courts. These constraints are weak, because judges enjoy long tenure and because the Supreme Court is largely unchecked. This is why responsible self-restraint is so important if judges are to hew to a compromising rather than enterprising mode of action. We can, however, supplement their self-restraint. Superior judges can contain their inferiors' power, and executives can deflect what courts demand. It is naive even today to ignore the chain of delay and litigation with which recalcitrant executives and legislatures can strangle judicial commands. Moreover, Congress can control jurisdiction, limit civil awards, restrict judges' sentencing freedom, and even change the standards for criminal guilt. Precisely because courts so often usurp democratic choice and justify their usurpation as democratic, the rest of government must begin to pull them back toward the political realm.[18] The internal exercise of responsibilities by judges is important, but it is becoming insufficient to protect liberty.

Rewards for excessive behavior by attorneys—inordinate delays, frivolous litigation, public grandstanding, and gross manipulation of facts—also need to be diminished. We cannot anymore expect lawyers to do this by themselves. Professional responsibility is insufficient here, given the nature of lawyers' market rewards and their immersion in ordinary politics. The circumstances that allow some newspapers to direct themselves to serious audiences and to set the tone for others work less well in law, where the few "permanent" big firms are not quite so dominant and where juries and local circumstances are so important. These firms do have a special role, but judges and legislatures must set and reset what counts as permissible behavior by lawyers. Some attorneys will see their responsibility in this larger light, of course, but it is especially judges (and the legislators and voters who choose and direct them) who must live in this larger light.

So, judges are central in restraining lawyers. Without their action an ethos of counseling and avoiding litigation in civil matters and achieving more vigorous prosecution in criminal ones will not take hold. The professional responsibility of attorneys is insufficient to push them individually to larger horizons, especially because they are concerned with their own wealth and success. Lightly regulated, untrammeled competition among lawyers may lead to good results for particular clients but not to fairer outcomes generally. Doing even their own jobs honestly without thinking of their context is not quite enough. The larger structure of government must channel legal competition so that it remains useful. The myriad of mechanisms by which attorneys bully, cajole, and delay can be controlled by vigorous judges or in advance by well-crafted law. One might argue that yesterday's restraints on advertising and other "unprofessional" behavior were merely controls that benefited the established. This shows all the more, however, that channeling an attorney's effort depends on courts and legislatures. They in turn rely both on the practical clash of responsibilities and on proper opinion about government's direction and role.[19]

We can restate and develop this last point as follows: When judges and legislators direct attorneys, they should foster actions that preserve and enhance their own capability for future effectiveness. Law generally should look to what permits and expands responsibility when choices must be made. A reasonable goal for a judge should be to give citizens no less freedom and responsibility in their own spheres than he demands in his. Responsibility is rooted in interests but reaches beyond merely balancing them. As rooted in interest, however, it is less subject to vapid persuasion or experts' impositions than are perspectives on the common good that pretend to ignore interests. Trying to advance equal freedom and responsibility through law does not depart excessively from self-interest or liberal common sense. Judges and lawyers, indeed, are especially able to consider larger standpoints in light of specific interests—to work from the particular to the general—because law's adversarial process is a clash of specifics. What resolves the specific clash fairly will usually be clear, as in criminal law. In novel cases, however, where the law does not offer immediate and complete direction, resolution should try to advance the scope and range of responsible freedom. This normally means that in areas such as finance, communications, health, and education, judges should look to the interpretation that expands the range of access to opportunities, the range of competition under applicable law.

REGULARITY IN LAW

No one can grasp fully what will secure freedom, because the future is subject to free action. This leads to my fifth point, which concerns the regularity we seek in law. We intend law to be suitably predictable, general, and transparent, so that similar cases are handled similarly and one knows more or less where one stands. Imagine if innocent actions suddenly are declared criminal today only to be found innocent again tomorrow, if the same actions are crimes when I but not you commit them, and if you cannot tell what law requires because it is befuddlingly opaque or contradictory. In such cases the virtues of the rule of law are vitiated or denied. Responsibility as accountability for the actions one intends cannot survive the chance and arbitrary.

One reason people object to "pragmatic" case-by-case judging, indeed, is the uncertainty this can create, even when laws are applied equally. Stability that sometimes leads to imperfect results in particular cases is preferable to seeking perfection on each occasion, because this attempt undermines predictability, generality, and transparency and opens the door to arbitrary actions. Moreover, stable law is more likely to reflect reasoned deliberation or even sensible balancing of interests than is constant judicial intervention.

Of course, rigid formalism might respond to changed circumstances improperly by arbitrarily fitting a strange or new case under an inappropriate category. New technologies never fit precisely under old laws. Misplaced generality sometimes is as harmful as treating each case afresh. Judgments that attempt to reach a prudent result in terms of the facts at hand can strengthen law's justice and even set the stage for legislative reconsideration of old issues. Generality, predictability, and clarity, that is to say, do not as such exhaust law's service to justice and therefore do not even exhaust law's ability to promote security. Moreover, strict rigidity diminishes the effective responsibility of those subject to unchanging law, although it makes it easier to determine guilt.

I conclude from this discussion that just as responsible action requires prudent flexibility in making law and executing it, so too does adjudicating require prudent action in enforcing and interpreting it. The prudent course here, however, normally is to place generality, predictability, and transparency beyond practical accommodations and certainly beyond arbitrary imposition. Judicial responsibility primarily means acting under the law while applying it. Political actions by judges, actions more legislative than judicial, need to be checked politically.

THE OBLIGATION TO OBEY

Still another factor increases the complexity of "law and responsibility," namely, questions about law's status. Is its obligatory force identical to being posited and enforced somewhere, say in our country or Nazi Germany, or is its obligatory force connected to its being (or striving to be) just by a more permanent standard? Even if we agree that a lawmaker must look to what is just, refracting his gaze properly through his country's constitutional limits and circumstances, should a judge properly leap to a standard outside the law? Or should he always stay within the posited law, seeking to carry out its intent in particular circumstances? We believe in the United States that we can justify our way of life through reason and not merely by imposition. That is, we believe that our legal goal—to secure responsible freedom—is not merely posited and accidental. Because we understand responsibility to be the heart of a character that can assert natural rights successfully, we cannot easily hide behind mere legal positivism. Yet, a country is not a philosophy treatise, so we cannot ignore law's positive, forcible, and necessarily arbitrary elements.

This issue is most immediate for us when we debate the standards for judicial interpretation of the Constitution, and I will develop it in this form. We might argue that the Constitution is similar to other laws and should be interpreted with whatever flexibility is proper to law generally. We might instead argue that it is a special case. We might say that we should not employ broad claims of right against legislation enacted by political institutions, or rather, that in considering constitutionality we should not defer to majorities as we might elsewhere. We might argue that the Constitution should be interpreted in the plain terms and practices of its own time, or rather, that we should use superior principles of justice—say, natural law, the founders' view properly grasped, today's common meanings, fancy contemporary philosophical views of justice, or today's reigning opinions about the boundaries for acceptable political action.

My opinion is that the responsible character our law seeks requires that the Constitution not be brought into play readily or interpreted as are other laws. Rather, judges need special circumstances to make it (rather than narrower statutes) directly applicable when they decide cases. Self-restraint usually is the best safeguard for rights, because the Constitution deserves reverence. Reverence means that we should not trivialize it by declaring a law or act unconstitutional if this seems marginally or even considerably better than accepting it. As we have said, law always is too gross and too rigid to encompass full justice. To ignore this necessary limit is to lose some of law's generality, clarity, and predictability by attempting a particular perfection that we cannot attain; the result will almost always be more arbitrary and less reasonable than when we allow the political deliberation and balancing memorialized in law to prevail. Even when courts habitually and therefore predictably override Congress, they are replacing political and constitutional government with punctilious extremism.

This constitutional reverence is not obscurantist and can be reasonable for still another reason. Deference to lawmakers permits at least one obvious constitutional action to prevail—the use of authority by elected officials. This authority needs countering only in unusual circumstances. These circumstances involve clear violations of equal rights as the founders understand them or clear interference by states or the federal government in each other's business.

"Clear" is not crystal clear, nor can it be. I mean only to suggest that a severe degree of confusion or violation should be visible before the court decides it might step in constitutionally. Less than this strips responsibility from public officials and opens us to the arbitrary or inflexible.

The way to notice a clear violation is to begin with the Constitution's original text and then current meaning, and to continue if necessary by considering the ground of this meaning. We can discover this ground by studying the thinkers on whom the founders drew. The advantage of this procedure is to combine as best we can the old and the good and therefore to recognize both the necessity and limits of posited laws. The Constitution is revered in the sense that it is used only hesitantly to reverse popular majorities and is interpreted with very special caution. When justices employ it to secure rights against statutes or to adjudicate disputes within government, they should defer to what the Constitution actually says. If they must go outside, however, they should go outside to the heights on which the founders drew, not to our own opinions or the modern lowlands.[20] Hewing to this procedure hardly resolves all constitutional disputes, but it does help preserve responsible action by individuals, the proper horizon for responsibility (the Constitution plus the thought behind it), and the responsible clash of institutions.

For these constitutional restraints to be observed, public and educated opinion is crucial. The clash of individuals and institutions is insufficient. Even the clash of those responsible enough to take on larger and larger tasks is not completely self-limiting when, for example, we deal with courts that can overturn elections. Self-restraint at that point requires good opinion (and more effective political checks.) Responsibility simply as a virtue is decisive but limited.

NOTES

1. One should (of course) carefully consider Tocqueville's analyses of these subjects in *Democracy in America*, especially those in the second part of the second volume.

2. See Walter Olson, *The Litigation Explosion* (New York: Dutton, 1991); Walter Olson, *The Rule of Lawyers* (New York: St. Martin's, 2003); Philip Howard, *The Death of Common Sense* (New York: Warner, 1996); Philip Howard, *The Collapse of the Common Good* (New York: Ballantine Books, 2001); and Richard Epstein, *Simple Rules for a Complex World* (Cambridge, Mass.: Harvard University Press, 1995). In 2003 there were more than a million lawyers in the United States (*Chicago Sun Times,* December 26, 2003, 52). The *Statistical Abstract of the United States* gives the figures for previous years.

3. Consider Martha Derthick, *Up in Smoke* (Washington, D.C.: CQ Press, 2002).

4. It is amusing and in its own way frightening to read intellectuals as intelligent as Richard Posner praising the sophists for their supposed pragmatism and decrying Plato for his . . . Platonism. (See his *Law, Pragmatism and Democracy* [Cambridge, Mass.: Harvard University Press, 2003].) A proper Socratic sentence for this injustice would be to sentence him actually to study, say, the *Gorgias* or *Protagoras* and not to rely so much on colleagues and secondary works.

5. Courts have moved to limit the punitive damages that can be awarded in lawsuits and have strengthened criteria for "expert" evidence.

6. Some of these concerns also move conservatives. Chief Justice Rehnquist has long complained about sentencing restrictions; William Tucker in *The Weekly Standard,* June 16, 2004 has praised some results achieved by trial lawyers.

7. Consider Aristotle's *Ethics,* Book V.

8. One can explore attorneys' codes in Norman Redlich, comp., *Standards of Professional Conduct for Lawyers and Judges* (Boston: Little, Brown, 1984).

9. The general strictures against excessive tort claims that misassign responsibility are in this regard correct. We see such strictures in books such as Howard's or Olsen's.

10. Consider the work of Aaron Wildavsky on the issue of risk, for instance, his *Searching for Safety* (New Brunswick, N.J.: Transaction Books, 1988). Economic marginalism considers matters too narrowly, because it demands too much attention to trivia and isolates decisions too much from character and the general course of life. Yet its perspective yields results that in some ways are similar to what I am suggesting. Moreover, its discussions of public goods, transactions costs, information and the like allow it to take serious steps on these matters, within its own devices. Richardson's discussions in *Democratic Autonomy* of cost-benefit analysis are interesting in this regard. (Whether government regulation in warranted areas should be highly directive or broadly encouraging is still another question.)

11. In fact, responsibility's breadth allows it to substitute for some of the breadth of justice as well as pride. This breadth covers any good one might imagine, all of which can be handled justly or unjustly.

12. See Aristotle on universal justice, *Ethics* V.

13. The difference in meaning, such as it is, is connected to this substance and, especially, to philosophical understanding.

14. The right and the fair are not identical. To be fair or fair-minded belongs to character, as does the disposition to do the right thing, although we normally describe people as fair-minded rather than as right-minded (and to be right-thinking is another matter.) This difference, however, does not involve areas one covers but the other does not. One can distribute any good fairly or correctly and perform any action in the fair or right way. There are additional differences.

When a meal is fair it is not very good, when the weather is "fair" it is either not very good or filled with sunshine, and a woman whose looks are "fair" could be average, beautiful, or merely pale. The sense of fair as mediocre sometimes echoes in the just as the fair: a "fair" distribution leaves none dissatisfied but might not be beautiful or just right. In this sense the just as the fair points to equality simply, or has in mind sensible terms for a proper distribution (all players deserve an equal World Series share) but not ones that fit best from every point of view (why not give more to those who performed best?). It is fair to divide goods equally among heirs, yet it seems wrong for the most needy, worthy, or loving not to receive more. Nonetheless, we should not overemphasize the difference here between the fair and the right. We might also call the heirs' equal portions "correct" or "right" but "unfair," and either the equal or unequal distribution might be "beautiful" and in this sense fair. I conclude, therefore, that justice both as what is right and what is fair concern what is fitting, proper distribution. It is not fair versus right but the multiplicity of grounds of ownership and connection that are crucial in different substantive views of justice. Our meanings reveal their openness as well as their precision.

15. Doing what is right as undeviatingly following the proper path exemplifies the "just so" as the exactly fitting in which exactitude itself takes on a life of its own apart from its purpose. To follow the law without being self-righteous, of course, also is to do what is right, and our terms "justice," the "justice system," and "justices" also remind of law and punishment, if less punctiliously than righteousness.

16. It is instructive to consider here the fifth book of Aristotle's *Ethics* and the third of his *Politics*.

17. It also necessarily brings about distortions in the direction of access through wealth of what would be fitting distribution of goods in terms of excellence.

18. See the large literature on deliberative democracy, much of it referred to in Richardson.

19. Responsibility rather than abstract theory is central in stating that role and defining it. Consider and contrast here Cass Sunstein, *Legal Reasoning and Political Conflict* (New York: Oxford University Press, 1996).

20. Were our Constitution not good, of course, one could not so easily recommend this procedure.

5

THE POLITICAL RESPONSIBILITY
OF THE MEDIA

The media in the United States have been under special scrutiny at least since the Vietnam War. Everyone then suddenly realized that journalists did not passively report events but shaped them and our attitude toward them. Television was especially praised or blamed for galvanizing opposition to the war; Spiro Agnew began the attack on the press that made his final downfall such a pleasure for journalists everywhere.

This scrutiny has lead to a number of propositions, or discoveries, about the media. Taken together, these opinions (which are not always coherent) define our current view. By reminding ourselves of them, we can begin to elucidate the central elements of the topic— the political responsibility of the media—to which I turn next.

One prominent discovery is that, in the United States at least, important journalists belong to what passes these days for an intellectual class. They resemble novelists, professors, and consultants. The typical journalist of fifty to a hundred years ago was more likely to resemble a private detective, often a dishonest private detective, than an academic who loves to bury himself in research warrens. Back then, one was trained to think of journalists as hard boiled, part of the lower- and lower-middle-class culture of (local) politicians, prostitutes, and policemen. These days, the typical journalist is likely to convey the mushy concerns of upper-middle-class angst: "hard boiled" is about the last thing one would think of calling the pampered products of our suburban high schools and pastoral colleges. Today's journalists may be a bit more cynical and shameless than their other well-educated friends, but they are basically nice guys, not tough ones. Where they differ from lawyers, physicians, and bankers, and resemble professors, not only in their work but also in their views is in their politics, which are to the left of other Americans, even well-educated ones. Polls show regularly that prestigious journalists vote more for Democrats than for Republicans and have views on social issues to the left of most Americans. Debates rage about whether this leads to bias in reporting. Looking from the right the bias is clear, especially when one considers the sneering tones of the *New York Times, Washington Post,* the three major networks, and National Public Radio, a special *bête noir.* From the left, one points out how journalists largely fell in line with the Bush administration after September 11, 2001, never challenging the United States radically while working for publishers and owners more conservative than they. In any event, whatever the truth about media bias generally, most agree about the liberalism of prestigious American journalists.[1]

A finding related to the discovery of a new class of leading journalists is that well-known, Washington-based, television-appearing reporters are more "elite," come from better schools, and make more money than their fellows. Everyone in the media these days is becoming the intellectual type I described above, but the Washington reporter even more so. There is reason to believe, however, that the wish and need of publishers to balance men in the newsroom with women and minorities will somewhat close the prestige (if not the income) gap. The diminishing distinctions among what the best and the next-best schools convey (so that Harvard and, say, the University of Michigan are almost unimaginably similar, seen from the viewpoint of a generation or two ago) will exacerbate these trends. Differences in ethos, education, and level of "contacts" will continue to decline. This, of course, will not make the most prestigious schools any less sought after, but it will mean that a good graduate of a good journalism (or liberal arts) school will often not suffer significant disadvantages. She will need to have gone to a decent school, however, because journalism has become so much a middle- and upper-middle-class matter.[2]

Differences in income, nonetheless, will be less easy to overcome, especially between those at the very top and everyone else. This is because of the second major discovery that we have made about today's media, namely, their increasingly close link to entertainment. This discovery is surprising to some—especially those who thought that the serious journalism of the Eisenhower and Kennedy years was all that journalism ever was or could be—and condemned by all. Television anchors and major reporters are stars, who are paid stars' salaries and attract the attention of gossips. Their "personal" lives are scrutinized constantly. Their "professional" lives are governed by popularity and likeability, not authority and respectability. They host and appear on shows the purpose of which is less to report the news than to make it. They write and edit in ways that merge the techniques of fiction with reporting, and of up-scale cinema with prosaic newsreels. The news and entertainment divisions of the major networks increasingly are intermingled; sometimes they are run by the same executives, often working on the same stories or products. The gulf between serious journalism and frivolous trash is now crossed with surprising ease. What started as a glorification of Woodward and Bernstein's reporting on Watergate has resulted in the increasing identification of the *National Enquirer* and the *New York Times*.

The third discovery is that, whatever their politics, reporters and editors are likely to let the imperatives of an interesting story govern their selection and presentation of facts. They remain passionately interested in scoops. They cannot wait for an election to end before announcing the winner—hence, they have invented exit polls. They cannot cover stories, especially political stories, except by reporting who is winning and who is losing, who is up and who is down. They are unable to sniff political rumors without soon sneezing uncontrollably into print. All this often overcomes the fact that the victim or villain of their story may be their friend, and the hero their enemy. Bill Clinton did not receive the unreservedly negative coverage the Right believed he deserved, but he hardly received the unvarnished praise he coveted.

A fourth discovery is that where big business, corporate moguls, and, especially, government are concerned, the serious media consider themselves to be "adversarial," always on the lookout for failure and corruption, always ready to defend citizens from their own representatives. The media are not part of the team but vaguely alien parasites whose constant complaining cleanses the "system" the way some ghastly bacterium helps with digestion. When a television network or newspaper departs from this adversarial posture (as many did during the Iraq and Gulf wars) and acts as an informed, questioning, but clearly patriotic citizen, others will be sure to condemn it.³

A fifth proposition is that the media primarily are businesses, much like any other business in their basic desire for profit, as this desire is modified by the trendy opinions or odd legal requirements of the day. This discovery has become less a matter for cynicism than for gentle sadness and nostalgia, or even deep worry and concern. Not a day used to go by in the United States without some graybeard lamenting the disappearing local newspapers or praising a responsible old hanger-on in Florida or Arkansas. Hardly a day goes by today without thumb-sucking about media conglomerates. Afternoon newspapers in America are increasingly rare because they do not make a profit and because national chains (and national newspapers) are replacing them. The result, so the proposition goes, is that bland information displaces both charming idiosyncrasy and careful attention to local political events.⁴ In this regard, the continued family control of the *New York Times* is the cause of wonder and even worship. The *Times* reported with a careful calibration of objectivity and reverence its owners' proclamation in 1990 that control was passing from one Sulzberger to another, letting us know that the new man was his own man but not too much his own man, crossing his *t* with a slightly different slant, as it were, but still in love with the old alphabet. Even this flattering story, "news" because continuous ownership of institutions such as the *Times* is now strange as well as important, was filled with detailed discussion of the paper's financial condition. When the new Sulzberger went a step too far in defending his executive editor in the face both of the Jayson Blair scandal and a general sense that the *Times* was becoming too cavalier about facts and too partisan for the newspaper of record, he apparently was pulled back by his family and corporation.⁵

A sixth discovery is that although journalism is at best an uncertain "profession," questions of responsibility and ethics are not simply ignored—on the contrary. Most major newspapers have ombudsmen (even the *Times* has one now), and most journalists are at some time in their career subjected to "ethicists," a peculiar monument to Americans' ability to make money from anything, including certifiable impracticality. The American press has become the greatest set of flagellants since the heyday of monasticism. No convention of Freudians can rival its orgies of self-analysis. Each time the press revealed something in the 1992 Democratic Party primaries and in the impeachment controversy that Bill Clinton would have preferred remain hidden, for example, it doubled its pleasure by telling on itself. Clearly, many of the media elite liked and (still like) Clinton, in whom they recognize themselves, and wished they did not have to harm him. Clearly as well, most decry the blurring of the difference between serious newspapers and scandal sheets, and the endless televised repetition of petty but "symbolic" events that has fueled political coverage from Edmund Muskie's teardrop in 1972 (or was it a snowdrop melting on his cheek?) through Howard Dean's Iowa rant of 2004 (or was it only an effort to reinvigorate his losing team?).[6] Most of all, everyone seems to believe that the media are discharging poorly their responsibility to help the electorate choose intelligently. Politicians, after all, can talk to the people only through the media, and whether this is good (because it sometimes deflects demagogic immediacy) or bad (because it allows any Perotian, Sharptonian, or Buchananoid demagogue to bypass constitutional forms), it means that the media are politically important.

Despite all their discussion, however, today's media masters do not know what their political responsibility is or how to live up to it. In fact, their understanding usually is still couched in terms of the people's need or right to know, so that discussions of privacy and publicity that arise about politicians such as Gary Condit are little different from those one hears about Michael Jackson. But we at least have discovered that the media know that they should be responsible, whatever this means to them.

A seventh proposition about the press is that the medium may indeed sometimes be the message. Although we talk of the media, we believe television affects us one way but radio and print another. Whether we are dealing with news or commentary, print clearly allows stories to be conveyed through reasoned reflection more easily than does television. The drumbeat of repetition that elevates one kidnapping, murder, or even a contested presidential election to the status of national obsession can more easily be avoided when reading the newspaper than when watching television. The notion that what counts is what is said and how well it is said, but not the mechanism through which it is said, seems oddly quaint. The immediacy and directness of television cannot be controlled or manipulated successfully by omnipotent reporters and editors. Rather, the immediate power of television images forces them—and every politician who wants to be part of the news—to conform to it. What counts is what makes an impact, and whatever makes an impact gets through in the same way—the jarring repeated image and its associated headline (the sound bite)—whatever its old-fashioned meaning or truth. Even when television attempts discussion, short bursts of clashing opinion drown out reflective conversation.

An eighth proposition is that whatever the rise in media conglomerates and decline in the influence of print, news outlets are increasing. Cable television, talk radio, and Internet websites allow people constant access to more and more sources. Perhaps this leads to welcome variety. Perhaps, instead, it allows us to concentrate only on narrow concerns and points of view. Conventional wisdom leans toward the second view, but no one is certain. In any event, although television and its images remain powerful, and although the effect of the Internet as a medium is still undetermined, choices are increasing, and the dominance of the three networks is declining.

The opinion that the medium (often) is the message is connected to the ninth proposition, that there is no objective truth to be reported in any event, or that it is impossible to discern even if it exists. All but the simplest facts make sense only within a context. This context is not predetermined but is created by the questions that editors and reporters choose to emphasize. This perspective then determines not only the meaning of facts but even which items in the passing flow can be recognized as facts in the first place. This notion of the relativity of facts is so powerful, indeed, that even courts seriously entertain the view that putting quotation marks around statements that were not actually said can add to the truth of a story, not detract from it.

If we sum up these propositions and discoveries, we can represent our current view of the media. The leading reporters are well educated, generally leftist, and enjoy upper-middle-class lives. They are aggressive defenders of the prerogative to write what they please but are aware of a responsibility (that they often ignore) not to say everything, and of a special political responsibility. This political responsibility is vaguely understood as letting the people know what is going on so that they can vote intelligently or control their government; letting people know the "truth" about government has come to mean distrusting it as an adversary. Whatever the media's sense of responsibility or political intentions, however, journalists also are governed by the imperatives of a good story and a successful business, within an atmosphere that increasingly identifies news with information and entertainment. The number of media outlets has increased, but the number of serious outlets that amalgamate opinion rather than divide it has declined, as has attention paid to them. Indeed, the effect of stories often is beyond anyone's control, because the mechanisms (especially television) for conveying news control the effect of a story more powerfully than does its intended content, however artfully produced. Television forces editors who wish to be successful to produce "news" that, step by step, becomes indistinguishable from entertaining information; it then turns out that endless rebroadcasting often controls a story's meaning more powerfully than what the producer is intending to say. A story's content, finally, even if its effect on the audience does conform to what is intended, is not objective, because every fact that is not trivial is relative to perspectives and points of view.

WHY MEDIA?

Our current view of the media, I believe, derives from our reigning opinions about equality, competition (liberty), responsibility, immediacy (representation), and objectivity. That is, it derives from today's grasp of justice, virtue, and thought; our view of the media (and their own behavior) belongs to our growing substantive egalitarianism, our often waning responsibility, and the strange way in which we grasp truth. This means that our current opinions point to the principles through which we should understand the media and indicate the difficulty of their current condition. Our recent discoveries are not completely incorrect, and the facts on which we base them are not simply phantasms. But they are not fully accurate, nor is their significance assessed properly.

Why do we have the media at all? Why do we allow private institutions such power? Why are they so little regulated? Why can new newspapers, and even new television stations, so easily come and go? This leeway is unusual among countries, even in the West. The answer, in America at least, is our wish to develop and preserve large areas of private or social power. Government is not constrained by individuals alone but by strong businesses and a strong press. But why do we want government to be contained? We want this in order to preserve our rightful freedom, our not being mastered or restrained by something or someone alien. To master myself responsibly (to freely execute and effect my rights) I must be limited as little as possible by what I do not choose. This requires education (enlightenment) and leisure (sufficient resources). Without these, I am directed by necessity and superstition, or the narrowness of my opinions. The exercise of rights liberates abilities and raises desires that lead us to conquer penury and to overcome superstition and the natural unknown; we advance enlightenment and plenty by allowing the effective exercise of each person's own authority. Freedom leads to greater freedom. This liberation requires, however, that the limits one does choose—government most obviously—do not become oppressive.[7]

Increasing freedom and controlling possibly oppressive government occur through institutions, not only through isolated individual actions. For, what could it mean to say that my freedom grows if I individually control no one else, even the criminal, in any way? Yet, how am I free if others direct me? Government that we legitimize by individual consent and election, government that we choose in common, is the first means for securing necessary yet dispersed control. A second mechanism is competition, not just the clashing we discussed within government and law but removing any area of life from exclusive dominance by a single class. Constructing and forming competitive businesses and institutions affords a scope for the responsible freedom to shape and control, including directing others for limited purposes, that does not concentrate control or rigidify the powerful into permanent castes or classes.

Seen in this light, concentration of media ownership and homogeneity of reporters and editors is undesirable not only because they restrict political debate but primarily because concentration limits the opportunities for various abilities to flourish; it is both insufficiently liberal and insufficiently democratic. Freedom means the liberation of possibilities responsibly to master, or direct; a regime that serves freedom is one that tries to enlarge and disperse this political spirit. Therefore, anything that restricts the opportunity to form a limited empire of one's own is as such harmful. If we think first of the media as a group of separate businesses and corporations, we see that concentrating and homogenizing it contribute to the same decline in the vigorous and equal exercise of one's own rights, the same decline in responsible mastery, that characterizes much of contemporary America. The chief way in which the media check political power is less through what they say and more by providing a place for contentious control that is not government control. From this point of view, whatever enhances innovative entrepreneurship in the media is good. Any solution to the media's problems that works against rather than with aggressive innovation will most likely do them and the country more harm than benefit. We therefore suspect that worthwhile efforts to deal with the media's irresponsibility about doing their job, their political effects, or their own future also will support entrepreneurial innovation.[8]

THE RESPONSIBILITY OF THE MEDIA

A responsible media is a media in which editors and reporters bend their efforts to completing their jobs successfully. But it also is a media in which at least some bend their efforts to completing common tasks that they no more than others are obliged to undertake. In this sense, they assume responsibility for the community as a whole and do what is necessary for the public interest.

What, then, is the job for which the media are responsible? To begin with, anyone can attempt to make a living by selling to others what purports to be news and serious political analysis. There is no reason to restrict these opportunities, given that control of government requires more dispersion of power, not less. Who could securely say that things would have been better in the past or would always be better in the future if, say, politically oriented radio talk shows did not exist? Perhaps they contribute to hysteria. But perhaps they call to account politicians whom other media do not want to call to account. One might argue that thinking about the press as a business inevitably means that everyone will seek the lowest common denominator in order to make the most money. But in fact some always choose to sell to an exclusive clientele. Perhaps it is easier to profit from this clientele once one gets the hang of it. More to the point, not everyone seeks to sell as much as possible to the widest possible audience, because it is not profit alone but power and control—freedom—that motivates free men in a free society. As long as some see that speaking to intelligent citizens and owning and operating institutions that influence these citizens gives one special significance, there is no need to decry each and every vulgarity in the media business. In general, a newspaper or television network's responsibility is successfully to convey news and political opinion to the audience it has chosen.

Do the media have any responsibility beyond simply doing their job? We often say that the significant media set the tone. This means that they limit what they might otherwise do in the light of considerations that are not instant and immediate. They decide what news is by deciding what is fit to print. Obviously, they do not do this in a vacuum, because they take some guidance from their audience. But they still need to decide for themselves. By choosing to emphasize some things—say, national affairs—and ignore others—say, rumors about the lives of political candidates—they define, for a while, what counts as respectable. A cynic might say that in doing this they preserve their business franchise, by, as it were, inducing others who wish to be respectable and significant to play a game with rules they do not control. But they also forego the pleasures and profit that come from being less serious. That is, they choose to be responsible, to pay attention to the broad conditions their own continued utility requires, and to enjoy the greater influence, freedom, and respectability that comes from this.

About what exactly are the significant media being responsible? The man who makes himself responsible often takes charge during a commonly recognized danger or necessity. With the media, however, we do not have a commonly recognized danger that responsible publishers and editors meet. Rather, we have a more general responsibility for the country and the profession. For the profession, the responsibility is to overcome the often hidden danger that the media will fall too far short of their best self. Their best self is at one with discharging their responsibility to the country as a whole. What is this responsibility? All citizens should be responsible, and some must be, because a responsible private life does not automatically guarantee public benefits. One always is tempted to let someone else do public things. Citizens must do the citizen's job of voting, obeying the law, and paying attention to public concerns. Those who run business enterprises and institutions must do the same, but generally they have no special public responsibility beyond this. This is not true of those in the media. A reporter, editor, or publisher who does his job still does not do well enough, because the media have a special, separate responsibility that is not guaranteed by making a profit in a law-abiding way: the media are the filter, and therefore should be a responsible filter, through which politicians talk and public opinion is formed.

Not everyone in the media can or should accept this responsibility to the same degree; to demand this would be to assume that "responsibility" is whatever everyone can accomplish more or less easily. But some must accept it fully. Yet, we cannot try to guarantee that anyone will do this, because we cannot guarantee responsibility without restricting or distorting it. This is why we often need quasi-aristocratic institutions such as the *New York Times* to assume public responsibilities that are not commonly visible. (It is also why we are so concerned when they appear to depart from those responsibilities or a sensible understanding of them.) Others can then sometimes be shamed into following. It is precisely those in the media who wish to take on public responsibility who define themselves as serious and significant by carrying out this wish.

How does this help us to understand what the responsible course of action actually is? The media's special responsibility involves the fact that citizens and representatives need knowledge of immediate affairs in order to do their jobs well. The job of a representative is to deliberate about the common good and seek to bring it about, within the competitive, entrepreneurial atmosphere of American politics. Informed, reflective, public opinion guides representatives' deliberation, and citizens' thought about who deserves their vote. The media's responsibility is to provide the kind of knowledge, the "news" we need for deliberation in a way that enhances the possibility of deliberation rather than of hasty, immediate, emotional decision. The public job of the media is to provide knowledge that appeals as much as possible to the head and not the heart. Deliberation is reasoned reflection, and reason, especially in a country such as the United States, is the surest ground for discovering common interests and healthy compromise, because it cannot be itself without meeting the test of free, open, discussion.

To perform this task, a responsible journalist must set things in context and explain them; must not run with the pack and give things more importance than he thinks they deserve; and must attempt to transform the reader's immediate response into a pattern of thoughtful consideration.

This fact that a responsible journalist must decide what is important and put things in context is not a license to engage in eccentric interpretation while still enjoying the luxury of being considered responsible. It is merely a reason to observe the ordinary injunction in practical affairs to know something of background and motives in order to comprehend a particular event. It also means that the responsible media mistake their place when they consider it their proper task to be government's adversary. Rather, the media belong to the mechanisms that keep the people and the government at a proper distance from each other. To set in context, to decline to take at face value what obviously is not given at face value, to provide time for deliberation, to distrust at first bold executive enterprise, are all ways that the media help to secure the common good. But to doubt, often on principle, that the media's political responsibility is to serve the common good is to mistake their necessary questioning distance for constant adversarial criticism. The danger in being merely adversarial is that the media exacerbate popular contempt for government (and for themselves) and do not think through the consequences of this contempt. This is the height of irresponsibility, not responsibility.[9]

I may sum up my argument by saying that politically responsible journalism means asking: What does a practically intelligent legislator or executive engaged in deliberation about ways and means—not a curious gossip—need to know? Politically responsible journalism means seeing and forming things rigorously from the public-spirited point of view. The key to responsibility is establishing public spirit as the horizon and perspective, not some set of universal standards taught by a theology professor. The most politically responsible in the media also will stand a good chance of being financially responsible, because they will win and hold a significant and important audience. Others can follow their lead by addressing their important political stories to the most complex and thoughtful within their standard audience, in this way elevating their entire audience.

OBJECTIVITY

It will come as no surprise that I believe fancy views about the impossibility of objectivity to be dangerous and mistaken. The fancier they are the more dangerous they are. In practice, most come down to an argument about the necessary politicization of the news or, indeed, all thought. But in fact one usually knows when one is giving the news a partisan slant; if one normally can control political partisanship, there is no reason to believe that supposedly hidden points of view of race and class cannot also be brought to light.[10] Of course, some even might perceive as bias a deep, pervasive, and unquestioned "preference" for freedom to slavery, virtue to vice, or wealth to poverty. It is reasonable on some occasions to explore these opinions, but responsible public-spirited journalism loses nothing by accepting these "preferences." Journalism is a practical endeavor that should seek to limit its biases in a practical way, not a theoretical endeavor that rests uneasily with whatever it takes for granted. Moreover, although a responsible journalist who tries to aid deliberation will seek to know and control his biases, one virtue of competitive media is that frankly or obviously partisan perspectives can easily be counteracted. Finally, the need to put facts in context and explain them does not prove that all objectivity is a dream. It is indeed true that many events stand out practically only when we know what they mean. But we often know enough about what they mean if we have uncovered the history and intentions behind them. We can grasp these causes by attending to the ordinary considerations of everyday life. What is important to a community when we consider it from a public-spirited point of view—that is, what is important to its survival and the justice of its way of life—is the ordinary and sufficient practical standpoint. This standpoint allows us to decide, in a publicly demonstrable and arguable way, what is significant and what events mean. Journalism belongs to this context of practical deliberation. Practical objectivity is not so hard to achieve, and a responsible journalist will seek to achieve it.

Similar considerations allow us to judge the notion that the medium is coming to overpower the message. This is a serious situation if it truly exists. Too much immediacy, too much directness, means insufficient time for reflection, for consideration, for deliberation. It means insufficient distance between one's practical reflections as a citizen and one's immediate reaction as a rich man or poor one, a father or son, a Catholic or Protestant. Immediacy overcomes the fine distinctions that allow others their own responsibilities and, therefore, their liberty. Our public affairs should be seen as public, not as the object of one's immediate private passions. It is so difficult to secure this distance in any event that when the media work counter to calm deliberation rather than in support of it, we are especially concerned.

It is an open question, however, whether the importance of television truly heralds a new era in the immediacy of events, so that direct reaction to images replaces reasoned reflection. It also is an open question whether the way the Internet and cable television allow us so easily to tailor our news sources to our views is so novel. Is the situation so different from what it was in the days of yellow journalism and party newspapers? Perhaps it is possible to control our reactions, to learn to distance ourselves from them as we recognize how false these reactions often are. Perhaps we can learn to act publicly on the images we see only when they are presented responsibly or validated in print or over time. Perhaps, in fact, the glut of images leads as often to apathy as to constant excitation. One wonders, indeed, whether the speed with which we all learn the news now, whatever the medium through which we learn it, is not the truer foe of the statesman's reasoned reflection than any medium or mechanism per se. Even here, however, responsible presentation and responsible political reaction to the immediacies of news often can win the day. The people's (and government's) refusal to be stampeded against the Iraq War during its rough start is one example and (from a different standpoint) the people's cool reaction to the incessant demands for President Clinton's impeachment and removal is another.

In any event, our political problems have more to do with our uncertain sense of responsible liberty and equality, our uncertain political direction, than they do with this or that mode of communication. Much as television and radio contributed to the fall of communism, for example, the power of freedom and the rulers' loss of belief that communism was just or profitable were more important. It is comforting, nonetheless, to remember that the media's immediacy can be turned to good ends.

NOTES

1. As for bias, the best argument on the Left is that the Right still talks as if conservative positions on radio and cable are not broadcast regularly. (See, however, the *Wall Street Journal's* editorial "A Media Watershed," September 16, 2004.) To deny bias in the major outlets, as many do, however, is disingenuous. The most subtle study of this matter, which makes this bias clear, is by David Brady and Jonathan Ma in the *Wall Street Journal*, November 12, 2003, A18. One might also read Bernard Goldberg, *Bias* (Washington, D.C.: Regnery, 2001); Bernard Goldberg, *Arrogance* (New York: Warner, 2003); and Eric Alterman, *What Liberal Media?* (New York: Basic Books, 2003).

2. One might also consider the education and career of Jayson Blair, whose fabrications led to the dismissal in 2003 of the *New York Times'* executive and managing editors.

3. Consider Kathleen Hall Jamieson and Paul Waldman, *The Press Effect* (New York: Oxford University Press, 2003), and Christiane Amanpour's claim that the press muzzled itself in Iraq and the discussion of her claim in the media (Peter Johnson, *USA Today,* September 15, 2003). See also the exercise in self-examination and self-criticism in the *New York Times,* May 26, 2004, of its

reporting about the existence of weapons of mass destruction in Iraq in the years immediately preceding the 2003 war in Iraq.

4. One might argue that the main national newspaper, *USA Today,* in fact has confounded expectations by becoming more serious, not less. But not too serious: it faced its own scandal in 2004, when it reported that its lone foreign correspondent was fabricating stories.

5. Consider, for example, James Squires, *Read All about It* (New York: Times Books, 1993).

6. Consider Jamieson and Waldman here, in which several examples are collected. The book's overall view of the press' influence is excessive, however, and some examples misstate the significance of facts that the press is then said to distort or frame peculiarly. This is perhaps caused by the subtle (but clear enough) sense pervading the book that the Bush-Gore loser was done in unfairly.

7. Mistakes about what rights mean (as I discussed earlier) and the utter flattening and equalizing of desires (and technological success in meeting them) threaten to obliterate our grasp of the limits we need for genuine satisfaction and freedom. I discuss this in my penultimate chapter.

8. This is not altogether evident, however; it is not simply true in law, for example, where the best judges should not be especially enterprising.

9. Consider the British judge's report criticizing the BBC's coverage of the government's statements about weapons of mass destruction in Iraq, *The Weekly Standard,* February 16, 2004.

10. One might consider here *Bias, Arrogance,* and other such books. There are, of course, limits to this self-recognition. Even subtle conservative and liberal slants are largely controllable, with effort. One might examine, for example the *Los Angeles Times* editors' recognition of subtle and not so subtle slanting of its coverage of abortion issues.

6

LIBERAL RESPONSIBILITY

PHILANTHROPY AND RESPONSIBILITY

I turn now to philanthropy, because properly understood it is a significant example of responsibly taking on tasks that belong to no one in particular. It is not often directly political (and strictly speaking it cannot be legally), but it stems from the same expansive disposition as does high public service. I will concentrate especially but not exclusively on philanthropy's place in helping those in need.

It is not unusual for philanthropists to help provide good things for public use. Museums and orchestras, libraries and schools, hospitals and shelters, all receive philanthropic support, and the communities that benefit recognize that they are receiving something of public value. It also is not unusual for philanthropists to be asked for this support; the days of worthy groups waiting patiently for the philanthropic angel to descend are long gone. Perhaps they never existed. What may seem a bit strange, however, is that the public at large, or elite opinion, expects philanthropies to meet "public needs" that are generally, or, more precisely, politically, stated. If there is something that the city or country no longer can afford to do, or, indeed, that the voters no longer want the government to do but that elite opinion still wants done, philanthropy, it is said, should step in. There are gaps to be filled in health and welfare, in housing and training. Surely, so goes the argument, philanthropy should try to fill them. If it cannot or will not, our needs and our resources will be misaligned.

This rather orthodontic model of philanthropy became especially popular when the philanthropic establishment broadcast its fears about the Reagan budget cuts of the early 1980s. It was difficult to avoid talk about the imperative to fill the budget gap or awful visions of what would occur if it proved impossible to do so. The model then largely faded from view in the blinding but directionless shining of the first President Bush's Thousand Points of Light. It reemerged when opponents of the Republican congressional victory of 1994 at once contemplated and lobbied against the likely meaning of this victory for social policy.

When President Clinton acquiesced to reduction and reform in social programs, the question of philanthropy's place in aiding the needy again took on new force. Among those unhappy about the change, the effort was intense to persuade philanthropists to fill welfare gaps that they believed (incorrectly as it turned out) soon would become massive holes. When the next President Bush took power a version of the issue again surfaced, this time in terms of whether "faith-based" groups should carry out or supplement government's programs.

In all these cases there is a prior question: Should philanthropists take their lead from government or elite opinion in the first place? I intend to address this issue by making a number of points and drawing conclusions from them. The points I make are meant to raise issues worth considering whatever one's perspective, and even if my conclusions are disputed.

Philanthropy and Private Action

The first point is that philanthropy is private activity. Any choice by a philanthropist to engage public needs should therefore be understood as precisely that—a choice. Choices should be practically reasonable and responsible or even noble, but they cannot be free and at the same time be defined primarily by government. The difficulty if we use the wrong grounds to encourage philanthropists to attend to the needy is that their aid comes to be seen as a legal or political requirement, subject to legal or political control, and not as a munificent decision. Wealthy philanthropists are more able than most to take on expansive responsibilities. For any philanthropist this may involve funding public needs or some other public good. But performing these responsibilities is not a legal necessity.

Philanthropy also should not be subject to contemporary views about "social responsibility" that seek to put ownership of resources at least partially in the hands of those affected by their use. These doctrines range from earnest notions of stewardship fashionable in philanthropic circles to bizarre teachings about property rights fashionable in law schools. Although a philanthropist's wealth may have been earned in particular places, it is a philanthropists' own intentions and understanding of his responsibilities, not legal obligations to others beyond contractual ones, that should direct his use of his wealth. Whatever concerns about a neighborhood or his employees that the owner of a factory, store, or theater wishes or needs to take into account, these concerns do not give employees or neighbors a property right in his business.[1]

Philanthropy and Dominant Opinion

The fact that philanthropists are private should govern how they treat opinions that purport to direct them. There are many possible goods that philanthropists might help provide, including education and art. Public needs in the sense of aiding the needy are among these goods but do not exhaust them. Given this breadth, and given that philanthropy is essentially private, philanthropists should not subject themselves to dominant currents of opinion that try to define for them a monolithic task or even a narrow number of them. Private activity brings public benefits primarily through competition, compromise, responsible judgment, and choice, not through rigid regulation and tutelary guidance, and this is as true of philanthropy as it is of the economy.

This point is easy to miss, because whatever one's views about generosity one believes these views to be suitable for everyone similarly situated, not merely oneself. It is a short step from this position to subtle and not so subtle imposition.[2] It is therefore almost always better to think about philanthropists in the plural than about philanthropy in general, for this calls to mind their peculiar interests and the down-to-earth sources of their wealth.

It is not enough that philanthropists keep away from a monolithic view of where to use their resources. As private persons, philanthropists also should cleave to their own understanding of the meaning and range of the areas in which they choose to be effective. A philanthropy's understanding should be its own, formed by itself, and its methods and governance should be appropriate to a private organization. This independence and effort is how a philanthropist expresses his own virtue, his own shaping of matters in terms of his character and judgment. A philanthropy is not an arm of the state even when it does what the state once did. If it tries to meet public needs it still should follow its own view, because responsible philanthropy is a goal of free government, not only a means employed by current administrations.

A philanthropist's own view should, of course, be well considered if he or she means to be excellent and effective and not merely arbitrary. But no "reasonable" view can be mandated. One may be quite upset when a foundation seeks to educate public opinion foolishly or mold public policy dangerously. Anyone can name a foundation he believes to be a repository of stupidity. George Soros's use of his wealth to promote what is in effect the legalization of marijuana is very unwise. But better this than that foundations should yield their judgment and independence.[3]

Private Action and Public Goods

To understand the kinds of matters philanthropists should consider, it is useful to discuss public goods. For although philanthropy is private conduct, the source of which is private wealth, it serves certain types of interests and activities. In particular, philanthropy deals with goods that are unlikely to be produced sufficiently or enjoyed properly if wealth is the only motive or the defining one.[4]

It might seem that if goods are not objects of profit, the only alternative is to provide them through government. A moment's reflection disabuses us of this view. Love and education in the family, religious faith, the quest for knowledge, refined art, music, and literature, care for the poor, attention to public affairs, national security, domestic safety, punishment of criminals, and public infrastructure all are things that a love of wealth alone would not let us produce or enjoy sufficiently. Yet, how many of these goods could be provided adequately or attractively by government? Speaking generally, of goods that are not obvious objects of profit, only those best provided through a monopoly of force are candidates for exclusively public provision.

We also should see that although the distinction between what is and is not suited to private markets is important and real, it is not hard and fast. Consider education. It is difficult to know what constitutes a proper education before one already has one, and for this and other reasons too many people apparently will not "purchase" as much education as they should. This is why private institutions are heavily subsidized with philanthropic gifts, and it is why some government funding of education appears necessary even if it is through vouchers. Yet, it is easy enough to imagine a largely market system that adjusted schools and curricula to people's private wishes and ability to pay. The difficulty today would be that the resultant education would likely not be good enough, especially for the children of the poor and uneducated. The public understanding and responsible character required in a country governed by equals would therefore suffer. But we cannot be certain of this, and some believe that a completely market system subject at most to government injunctions about minimum requirements would suffice.

The place of philanthropy is to help with goods that do not benefit from a monopoly of force yet seem ill provided by the motive of wealth. (I say "help," because philanthropies do not produce anything. At best, they are outstanding examples of generosity.) High art and serious education need nonmarket help, for example, to the degree that respect, honor, study, and appreciation, not immediate utility, are required to secure and understand them. Government action in education and art is imperfect because the tendency of politicians to politicize support makes government an unreliable or even dangerous instrument on which to depend. The help too often comes with restrictive strings (say, affirmative action), is distributed through wasteful formulas (say, geographically balanced spending), or relies on dubious or narrow-minded "experts." Private philanthropy, given its variety and taken as a whole, is a sensible supplement to what artists and educators must nonetheless largely do for themselves.

Philanthropy and the Needy

As I mentioned in my earlier list, care for the poor is among the goods that the wish for wealth does not satisfy fully. Wealth is a necessary condition of philanthropy, of course, and our long-term prosperity helps explain the historically high standard by which we currently evaluate poverty and need. Our prosperity would not exist, moreover, were it not for the motive that wishing for wealth provides once the energy of self-interest is connected to the responsible spirit and institutions of democratic liberalism. Nonetheless, this wish does not furnish sufficient motive to distribute resources to those who cannot work. Government is the obvious court of next resort. But government suffers from significant weaknesses in aiding the poor.

Its chief difficulty is that aiding the poor is as much moral as material, and in the long run more moral than material. Government is ill suited to provide such aid directly or even indirectly to supervise it. Constitutionally, Congress and the states cannot make laws that establish religion. The present meaning of this injunction is an often arbitrary series of do's and don'ts, the strange result of years of shifting Supreme Court decisions. Whatever loosening of strings that might occur as the Court twists and turns in future interpretive frenzy, it is unlikely that it could permit government support of religion that would suffice for the moral task of aid to the needy. Beyond this, I doubt that a government-led moral crusade could free itself from the usual political debilities. There is more to be done politically than often is thought. Divorce, for example, is now too easy to obtain, and marriage's central connection to rearing children is increasingly ignored. But, on the whole, aggressively "moral" government might well shift between questionable attempts at monolithic imposition and improper equalizing of moral points of view and ways of life.

The main public benefit that philanthropy provides in treating public needs is precisely its greater freedom to attend to morality. It need not concentrate on the material alone, and it is not subject to legal entitlement. But philanthropies are not institutions that offer moral training and ethical care. At most they can help the religious institutions and the like that link training and subsistence to moral discipline and healthy character. Aid through such institutions, where it is needed and where a philanthropy chooses to furnish it, is triply appropriate. It deals with the still too neglected moral or "cultural" concerns that belong to the problem of poverty; it is furnished through institutions that embody the responsible discipline they are encouraging and demonstrate motivation beyond the merely economic; and it does not duplicate the job training or employment that government or the market can provide as well or better.

Responsible Philanthropy

I mention responsible discipline because it helps provide a moral standard for philanthropy's helping those in need and for social action generally. Responsibility is what one would like to engender among the needy wherever it does not already exist. Indeed, we are arguing that responsibility is what one would like to foster among citizens generally, not least because they will then devote themselves more fully to institutions that help those in need, though not only for that reason. The disposition to do your job well, to bring it to a successful conclusion, to secure your future effectiveness, and to then take on burdens that do not belong to you in particular but to your neighborhood, community, church, and country—this disposition is something properly to be sought for others and displayed in oneself. Without responsibility it is hard to imagine how equal rights will be defended, public spiritedness developed, or economic self-interest vigorously or intelligently pursued.

Responsibility, as we have said, links character not to a class structure of assigned roles and professions, nor even primarily to conscience and religious teaching (although it clearly can be compatible with these), but to an abiding respect for the equal rights, freedom, and self-reliance of individuals. It celebrates the primacy of these individual qualities even in the midst of taking on tasks for and with others. In this sense, it differs from the view of responsibility that is endemic in communitarian rhetoric and in the usual call for philanthropic and corporate responsibility. For there, the emphasis is on what one owes to others, on the willingness to apologize, on the purity of intentions, and on the excesses of selfishness. The emphasis is not primarily on responsibility as the self-respect from which what is good for others as well as for oneself might arise.

The practical difficulty is that it is hard to foster responsibility in others without being tempted to diminish it in them. One becomes afraid that tasks will be done poorly or not at all. The tendency then is to take the responsibility away and to do the job oneself—and this contradicts the original goal. This difficulty, however, is not insoluble. To return to the example of education, school vouchers can at once increase the responsibility of those who receive them and effectively increase learning. But for this to occur, a system of vouchers must exist within a structure of timely help and information, and of flexible, attentively managed schools.

Speaking generally, coordination between the qualities that we need politically and those that we have is always incomplete. Freedom and wealth do not guarantee and sometimes work against the conditions of their own prosperity. It is a delusion to think otherwise, as if there could be a full and easy correspondence between naturally good but imperfect things and all our conventional practices. Responsibility can be supported coherently by freedom (and wealth) because they usually can be made to advance each other. Responsible character helps free individuals accumulate the goods we need to satisfy our desires, and it often presses us onward as we try to take charge of more and more. Nonetheless, wealth and the conditions we require for future success do not always or automatically advance each other. Disciplined and responsible work can lead to wealth, but wealth can then lead to indiscipline and immoderation. Responsible public spirit can help to secure citizens' political freedom, but the freedom won requires continuing moral and intellectual education about its effective, responsible, and excellent use. For, freedom does not provide sufficient guidance about how best to use or preserve itself, and wealth alone is inadequate to supply this lack. People who are satisfied with their abundance and comfortable in their lack of restraint, moreover, can become unwilling either to seek or accept the requisite teaching.

Because the wish for wealth does not allow us sufficiently to produce or enjoy many worthwhile things, including properly expansive responsibility, public and private institutions in addition to competitive markets are necessary. These institutions—responsible government, law, media, homes for scholarship—can deflect freedom and expand it by forcing and encouraging it to be responsibly refined and enlarged. These institutions include responsible philanthropies. When a philanthropy chooses to help the needy, its central goal should be to foster responsibility (and the freedom that is coordinated with it) where it does not exist sufficiently. In fact, to advance responsibility also is, and should be, a driving purpose of philanthropic programs (and of government) in elementary and secondary education, in drug-abuse prevention, in reducing out-of-wedlock births, and the like. It is even the purpose of programs the direct function of which is to relieve economic disaster, for the intention of these programs is to put people back on their own feet.

Some Limits of Philanthropy

Whatever philanthropists do to meet public needs, they should not forget their (other) traditional fields of funding. Fine art and music may not be needs, but will they be supplied sufficiently either by government or by the exclusive motive of wealth? Higher education is not an immediate requirement of the poor, but will it be produced fully by politics or profit? Sensible understandings of limited government, of the difference between equal liberty and equality simply, of individual rights as opposed to group entitlements, of the substance of moral and intellectual excellence and responsibility, of the conditions for the creation of wealth—are all these public needs? They certainly are not if "needs" mean minimum requirements for economic well-being and, therefore, ethical independence. Yet, they surely are important goods, or even needs, if by needs we mean the conditions for healthy public life and for human achievement. The state of art and of higher and civic education in the United States does not lead one to say that markets can support without help what is intelligent, fine, and refined. As with the media, there usually is too good a return for the foolish, the vulgar, and the mediocre. The situation of government generally, and especially today, does not suggest that public mandates encourage sufficient excellence and responsibility. It therefore sometimes takes philanthropic spending to supplement the ordinary and spontaneous support of serious art, thought, and education.

Conclusion

I conclude by summarizing my major points. Philanthropy is fundamentally private, and philanthropists should therefore follow their own understanding of which areas to support. They should not bow to public or elite opinion, or to government, although a prudent philanthropy should work to make its opinions practically and ethically reasonable. The central areas of philanthropic concern involve specific kinds of goods, namely, those insufficiently produced or enjoyed when wealth is our chief motive. There are many such areas, ranging from refined art, higher learning, and civic education to such public needs as aid to the poor. If a philanthropist chooses to aid the needy, this aid should concentrate on qualities not reached effectively by government, most obviously the development of character. This suggests that aid would best be given through institutions that are religious and moral at their core. One useful standard for the outcome a philanthropy might seek in dealing with public needs is to help to develop responsibility, because, understood correctly, responsibility sums up traits of character that at once benefit others and are suited to individuals who are citizens of a country based on equal rights and voluntary action. Philanthropy itself expresses the responsible disposition to take on tasks that belong to all and therefore to none in particular.

RESPONSIBILITY AND LIBERAL EDUCATION

I turn next more directly to responsibility and education, a topic of obvious importance. If our education is mediocre, equal rights will be poorly understood, the disposition to exercise them responsibly will be ill-developed, and institutions that attempt to direct self-interest intelligently will be misconceived. Teaching, moreover, itself expresses individual and professional responsibility. Beyond that, to consider education carefully is to come to grips with responsibility's limits.

Education does not occur exclusively in schools. Families, churches, and the media all are involved. Here, however, I examine formal education, in particular higher education, and within higher education, liberal education.[5]

Few people who think about today's liberal education fail to recognize that it suffers from many weaknesses. They disagree, of course, about what these difficulties are and about how significant any single one is. My diagnosis is similar to that in books that decry the political correctness, narrow-mindedness, and distorted view of truth that dominate much of the humanities.[6] I do not intend to repeat this diagnosis, however, but to discuss what liberal education is, what distinguishes it, and what the responsibility is of educators and intellectuals generally. My basic point is that the first and, in a sense, the final responsibility of intellectuals is to secure and improve as best they can in their own circumstances the conditions that make their enterprise possible. Self-interest fully and properly grasped will lead to a fundamental moderation from which even the occasionally radical action might appropriately follow. Ultimately, this requires that intellectuals consider two things—their own enterprise at its peak or in its best light, and the effects on each other of intellectual effort and a reasonably free and virtuous political life. The difficulty with most intellectuals and professors is their failure properly to consider these two phenomena.

Liberal Education and the Professions

I begin by considering liberal education as a profession or activity we choose as we do any other. Seeking wealth does not ensure liberal education's existence, but at least some of liberal education's elements are attractive enough that a market for it will exist. Moreover, responsible philanthropists will support it.

Perhaps, therefore, whatever we believe ails liberal education can be ameliorated sufficiently by private choice and competition, together with philanthropic support. This view must be at least partially true, for how else could we explain the islands of excellence, or at least sanity, that we see and the continued presence of much (or at least some) that is familiar and good in the liberal arts? The situation is similar to what we find in fine arts or high culture overall. Moreover, even if competition and responsibility are insufficient to push the liberal arts altogether in the right direction, perhaps the efforts of scholars and institutions who see their task and audience in the most exclusive terms can lead the rest.

The limit here is that none of these practices will be sufficient unless we understand substantively and subtly what is good about the liberal arts. Matters are easier in other areas. The continued authoritative exercise of individual freedom calls for the diligence, attention, and care that make up the habit of responsibility. As is true of grasping the need to accumulate property, however, recognizing the importance of ordinary responsibility or industriousness does not call for special comprehension of what actually is good or of how desires should be measured and ranked. Being responsible and seeking property largely replace this need. Responsible effort under laws that protect equal rights is mostly neutral to the desires it satisfies.

We see something similar in our politics, law, and journalism. Thinking and acting successfully from the political viewpoint of responsible enterprise and compromise are no mean tasks. They require that one place oneself in and try to secure conditions of effectiveness. They work within the horizon of securing citizens' rights, however, so they do not require statesmen to understand subtly the qualities of each activity in their countries and how they fit precisely into an organized whole.[7] To be politically responsible, journalists need know only enough to assume the standpoint of responsible politicians, again within a common understanding of equal rights. This is not simple, for it also demands a sense of what secures and protects the profession as a whole, but it does not require a complex grasp of truth. When lawyers are guided by rigorous judges, they too will act in a way that supports their profession, within an understanding of justice as what secures equal rights.

With the liberal arts, however, we need deeper effective knowledge of the good at which we aim. Here we come upon the limits of responsibility, though less quickly than we might imagine or fear. The disposition and intelligence to execute one's rights effectively do not tell us much about what goods to desire and enjoy. Together with sensible institutions, however, responsibility does go surprisingly far; not only the journalist, attorney, or physician but even a vigorous president of a good college can be markedly successful even if he takes for granted and hardly thinks about the worth of the liberal arts or education generally, and works within conventional notions of them.

But he will make mistakes—he will do harm—if what he supports is not the real thing, and it is difficult here to know the real thing.

This problem is still more pressing for the teachers and scholars directly responsible for conveying and advancing serious thought. Moreover, when we must address the meaning of liberty, responsibility, and equality explicitly, securing and prosecuting them within the usual practical understanding falls short. Teachers, judges, and statesmen, however, do sometimes need to handle them explicitly. The liberal arts are central in guiding our precise understanding of equal rights, responsibly free choice, and what is good; when we pursue them we cannot responsibly avoid confrontation with the good at which they aim.

Justifying Liberal Education

I will explore liberal education further by considering how, beyond there being a market for it, it is justified. After all, it produces nothing and serves directly only a few. We find one clue in the motive behind philanthropic support. We have said that the expansive responsibility taken on by some free men, such as philanthropists, seeks to place itself within, and to shape, wider and wider worlds. Liberal education is one entrée into worlds of greater freedom and responsibility than we usually experience, because it reveals and may then loosen the shackles of ignorance, narrow horizons, and dogmatic superstition. Our liberal entrée into this world is subject to grave mistakes and difficulties, however, unless we see more adequately how and why liberal education becomes necessary, and address explicitly the topics with which it deals.

The first element that clarifies the need for liberal education involves the difficulty that practical activities face when forced to defend their purposes and ends. They lack the resources to accomplish this themselves. The physician as such cannot, simply by virtue of his profession and skill, show why, when, or where health is good. When should death be risked and when not? The producer of goods at any level, from a shoemaker to a Gates, cannot, through his distinguishing skill, clarify the propriety of the goods he produces. What purposes do they serve? How defensible are these purposes? Do his products serve these purposes appropriately?

The need to think about such questions is at some point inescapable. But are they simply unconsidered in practical affairs? No. They are answered implicitly by a community's way of life—by its political understanding of the common good and the place of activities, professions, and citizens in this good. However: can citizens, let alone passing administrations, genuinely grasp and defend our way of life? Can we defend our opinions from challenge? Is a life devoted to free effort best, or rather, one grounded in religious devotion, political rule, military honor, or romantic sloth? To the degree to which we cannot answer these questions (let alone the question of what I should choose for myself), the political community falls short of knowing what it, and all the practices and professions within its ambit, sometimes most need to know. Liberal education first demonstrates its significance as reasoned discussion of the fundamental purposes from which other activities take their meaning, individually or in common. Our practical excellence is threatened at its core if, as so often happens today, educators misunderstand and discuss irresponsibly wealth, health, virtue, beauty, and truth, and the rights, equality, liberty, responsibility, and institutions that order and define our way of life.

This defense of the need for liberal education is insufficient, however, because it considers liberal education to be ministerial, the first servant of the practical world. A truer understanding of liberal education needs to ask how it is its own reward, an end in itself. A proper understanding of liberal education explores whether it is itself a beautiful and attractive—perhaps the most beautiful and attractive—human possibility and therefore most eminently, if not most immediately, useful.[8]

Here we discover that liberal education distinguishes itself from other activities by most completely examining and exercising what is distinctive to human beings. Other education primarily makes up for our deficiencies as animals—for our lack of rigid limits in food, sex, clothing, and shelter. But liberal education employs our human traits for distinctively human purposes; it experiences through our reason the fundamental causes and structures of things and cultivates leisured enjoyment of our feelings, as reason and speech inform them. Liberal education shapes and teaches us to enjoy for their own sake both intelligence and our unique passions, the love of the beautiful, the sense of the mysterious and awesome, the sense of the ridiculous.

Liberal education therefore justifies itself in the last analysis because it properly employs our capacities when we are at leisure. Playful leisure is superior to all serious activity, even great statesmanship, because it uses for our unique ends the capacities that serious activity intends to preserve and support. It defends itself in the next to last analysis by helping to guide and elevate serious activities and serious techniques—all seriousness is for the sake of and founded on something beyond itself. To put this in the most accurate traditional sense: liberal education forms man's distinctive liberality or openness; it expands and shapes the soul. To continue to educate oneself liberally is the central goal of a lifetime. We are fortunate today that it can be the most immediate and urgent task for so many for at least a few years.

Liberal Education's Unity

Have I not made liberal education too consistent? It comprises the humanities, the social, and the natural sciences. These elements do not obviously belong to a well-formed whole. The first and most thoughtful raising of this question of disharmony belongs to the ancients who initially discovered liberal education; it is the question of the relation, the quarrel, between poetry and philosophy, where philosophy comprises the subjects of mathematics, physics, and biology as well as its own unique subjects. This quarrel is most beautifully and most amusingly developed in Aristophanes's *Clouds* and Plato's *Symposium*. Leading physicists of the recent past have considered it, and it once was familiar as the debate between the two cultures.

The elements of the quarrel concern the relative rank of the activities that constitute what is distinctively human. This is to say, however, that intelligent contenders do not debunk one or the other side completely. Any "scientific" debunking of the philosophical elements of politics and morality or of the historical and literary experience of human greatness founders on the fact that the natural sciences are human activities that need human justification. Any debunking of the physical study of nature or of mathematics thoughtlessly eliminates an entire area of experience of the beauty of truth and form. The possibility of purely encountering and discovering what is not human is a unique human gift; properly speaking, the sciences are not inhuman. The divisions among those who love knowledge and beauty do not in the last analysis detract from the essential unity of the life of the mind or from liberal education's purpose as the attempt to express and develop our excellent and distinctive capacities.

Liberal Education's Danger

Nonetheless, the chief danger to today's liberal education lies within liberal education itself, because the kind of defense I am sketching is now rarely made. Our liberal education has lost its sense of direction and is irresponsibly divorced from the conditions that secure and justify it. Some defend it as valuable but only because they value it traditionally and their values are no lower than anyone else's. Others see it as the expression of our dominant Western culture, no better than other cultures, however vicious or willfully illiterate they are. Still others, who benefit from positions in the liberal arts, believe them to be a sham but are happy to profit from their hypocrisy. Their understanding usually stems from unthinking attachment to the opinions of thinkers such as Nietzsche or Heidegger, with whom, of course, they would not have even their slight acquaintance were it not for liberal education. These false positions cannot defend liberal education properly even when they try, because they do not consider the true necessity of educated understanding or the true dignity of cultivating the mind.

An understanding conceived in terms of the most beautiful and attractive human possibilities, however, faces its own danger, namely, degeneration to rigid philistinism or even narrow political control. One of liberal education's great virtues is to soften this rigidity. The view that values and cultures are equal, and the resultant understanding of liberal education as just one more arbitrary choice, may leave liberal education without a firm ground but, at least apparently, it is faithful to human openness, contingency, and indefiniteness. Yet, when liberal education understands itself properly as the expression of reason it can save this contingency without destroying itself. By putting into question human ends, expressing what is distinctive about human beings, and dealing with the radical openness of choice, it cannot properly become dogmatic. The attempt to know the fundamental causes of things and to discover what is beautiful is as such a continual awareness of our incompleteness.

Still, the attempt to know cannot understand itself (the liberal arts cannot truly be open and liberal) without also recognizing the limits and distinctions between the human and the nonhuman. The liberal arts cannot be themselves without asserting their own dignity and responsibility, and their own dignity is a kind of superiority. They exercise the distinctive and therefore the freest in man, and they do this by studying the highest, the most fundamental natural possibilities. The liberal arts at best, therefore, do teach one to be moderate and not improperly dogmatic, but also not excessively modest or timid.

The danger to the liberal arts that arises from the possible excessive modesty or dogmatism of their defenders is not the only current danger. The liberal arts are essentially playful, dedicated to knowledge and beauty, not to serious use. They therefore face the danger of being seen as frivolous, in a sense the opposite of the seriousness inherent in responsibility. They may thus seem no more important than any other frivolity. Here one might be tempted to concede the point and merely argue as we have that serious pursuits—earning a living, ruling a country, fighting a war, securing health—are all ultimately for the sake of leisure and the use of leisure. But this is insufficient, for the playful and leisured are superior to the serious only when they fully exercise our capacities of reason and speech, and employ the senses—hear the music and view the art—most informed by these capacities. The liberal arts cannot be themselves without defending their superiority to frivolous entertainment.

The liberal arts also are distinguished from the merely frivolous because they study the goals that practical activity serves. Only in terms of the powers, possibilities, and capabilities that we uncover in the liberal arts can we properly appreciate practical skills and pursuits in their own excellence. Merely frivolous activities furnish no grounds for such appreciation; in terms of what the liberal arts uncover they are less significant, less human, and less responsible than properly informed practice. This is how the liberal arts answer the frivolous—say, bowling, either together or alone. It also is the answer—as we suggested at the beginning—to possible disdain from the serious and technical.

This argument does not negate the fact that in principle liberal education is not wholly compatible with political and moral life. Political communities are enclosed in opinions about freedom and justice. This is healthy within limits, if the opinions they take for granted are healthy. Practical affairs require artificial limits for their successful, responsible conduct. But the liberal arts challenge these limits. Are they not, then, harmful?

This issue is a species of the classic problem of the relation between philosophy, taken in its broadest sense, and politics, taken in its broadest sense. Liberal education can lead to salutary moderation of dogmatic political and moral opinion, salutary precisely because these are dogmas and opinions. But such moderation is harmful unless liberal education also tempers the possible contempt for what we must take for granted politically and morally. Liberal education opens the limits of everyday opinions; it moderates but also threatens to overcome them. When thoughtfully pursued, however, it also moderates our expectations concerning political and moral perfection. At best, therefore, it allows us to reunite with what is good within a community, now understood more fully. Liberal education is compatible with the responsibly executed equality of rights, even though it cannot perform its own task well without explicitly examining its purpose and practice. At its worst, however, our liberal education exacerbates the easy relativism and license that substitute for responsible liberty by understanding itself and all else in the flaccid terms I mentioned earlier.

Does not liberal education at its most responsible suggest that it is the province of the few? We cannot simply deny this, if liberal education ought not to fear making distinctions. The liberal arts in a democracy must tolerate all who are capable of them and many who are not. As much as possible, however, they should welcome them on their own terms. Democratic openness allows greater entrance to the liberal arts than do other regimes today. This is a significant opportunity, but it makes it peculiarly difficult for genuine art and thought to hold their own here and now. What responsible teacher of the liberal arts has not considered this danger in his teaching and work?

My mention of democracy leads to the final problem of today's liberal arts. This problem is that they, or some of them, have become too useful. Rather than simply appearing to be a danger to political and moral life, to serious concerns, and rather than needing or being able to justify themselves as the studies that consider the sources of the meaning of practical affairs, they appear to be extraordinarily useful—but still subordinate. This is a version of the ancient quarrel between philosophy and sophistry. We must distinguish the liberal arts from the concerns and products of the advisors, the research organizations, the translators of liberal education to technical utility. Liberal democracy not only desires to spread a version of the liberal arts but also seeks to (and must) use its products. Liberal democracy is coordinate with enlightenment. We must therefore defend natural and social science from becoming mere technique and the arts from becoming mass productions, and the outlandish idiosyncrasies that merely negate these productions. The liberal arts today face the unique dual danger of being useless and in another way too useful. This is a subject of my next chapter.

NOTES

1. Insofar as "social responsibility" means or involves corporate ethics, the true question is how a business can be forced or encouraged to attend to the general conditions of its own success. I believe I have discussed the general options sufficiently while discussing law and journalism: namely, the individual virtue of responsibility, competition, differentiating among (market) leaders and followers, punishment, and judges or other regulators. My argument in this chapter will add to but not center on these discussions.

2. Of course, one might try to persuade misguided philanthropists to correct themselves or discuss with philanthropists of good will where their giving could be most effective. The key words here are persuasion and deliberation, however, not hectoring and humiliation, and the persuasion needs to consider specific circumstances, not just a general point of view.

3. Similarly, the boards and managements of philanthropies should attempt to follow the intentions of their founders even after these founders are gone. Responsibly following intentions requires judgment, because circumstances change. Basic intentions, however, are easy enough to state and should form the

continuing purpose of foundations. So, although judgment is necessary, there is not much reasonable room for deviation if a foundation's original goals are clear and well described—say, to support funding for arts and music, not health and welfare, to support ideas and programs that advance limited, not collectivist, government, or to support study of political and economic principles, not funding for concrete operations.

4. Consider Aristotle's *Ethics*.

5. My earlier discussion of the media, upcoming examination of technology, and brief remarks about public education and social science supplement what I will say in this section.

6. See, for example, Dinesh D'Souza, *Illiberal Education* (New York: Free Press, 1991), and Charles Sykes, *ProfScam* (New York: St. Martin's, 1988). The best of these books is Allan Bloom's still indispensable *The Closing of the American Mind* (New York: Simon and Schuster, 1987).

7. Our representatives are not orchestra leaders, composers, or Platonic political scientists. The better ones understand the democratic character, not each thing that free men do in detail.

8. This suggests that the proper understanding of liberal education cannot defend each and every activity that goes by its name.

7

RESPONSIBILITY AND BIOTECHNOLOGY

I look now at the question of responsibility and technology, especially biotechnology.[1] This issue is urgent, because we soon may be
able to change our characteristics and the conditions under which
they flourish. How should we use this power? Responsibility is a
defining element in liberal democracy, so it also is central in understanding how to employ technology properly and guide it politically.
The hackneyed injunction to use technology responsibly, I will argue,
is more telling than it knows. It proves to be insufficient, however, because guidance also requires that we think through more explicitly
than we do in practical liberalism the nature of the ends and goods
we enjoy and the limits of responsibility itself. By discussing technology and, especially, biotechnology, I therefore will develop themes I
raised at the conclusion of the first chapter and in the preceding one.
I will place liberal responsibility in the broad framework of human
ends, goods, and choice.

TECHNOLOGY

Americans are raising significant questions about cloning, stem-cell
research, and genetic manipulation. How should we regulate these activities? What moral limits should guide the regulations, or our private choices? What do our new powers suggest about the conditions
of human happiness and excellence?

These questions are now visibly public and political, involving
presidential speeches and congressional deliberation. The more clois-
tered views and procedures of physicians and bioethicists over the past

thirty years have set much of the direction for debate and choice, but we are today placing professional judgments in a wider political context. Current discussion, moreover, often reaches back to books such as Huxley's *Brave New World*, thinkers such as Francis Bacon, and our history of regulating dangerous technologies, such as atomic energy. We see or sense that bioethical issues are not merely scientific or even political but that the power and presence of technology is endemic in our way of life.

I therefore will begin discussing bioethical questions by looking at technology generally. My intention is to think through what is genuinely novel about it. I then turn to biotechnology more directly.

What is technology, and why should it concern us? One view is that it simply stands for the results and methods of our mind put to practical use. More specifically, it is the organized use of mind to meet physical or economic needs. So, shoemaking is as much a technology as farming, which is as much a technology as medicine. One can distinguish these from human inventions such as political science or poetry that do not manipulate material directly. Or, one can include these.

From this standpoint, technology is as old as history or, at least, as old as the Greeks, who became able to separate many natural ends and means from divine direction. Our genetically altered pigs and corn are just the latest steps in farming know-how. Antibiotics are leeches that work. Shoemaking has hardly advanced at all. This continuity also would mean that today's technological issues are not especially novel.

The second view is that ordinary arts and crafts become something distinctive enough to call Technology, once we self-consciously turn the powers of modern mathematical physics to practical use. On this view, modern technology begins seriously once we start to fly, use telegraphs and telephones, and make weapons and drugs systematically according to general physical and chemical principles. A decisive break has occurred between what we do now and past human invention.

This view is powerful and worth extended consideration. Yet, it proves surprisingly difficult to put one's finger on just what is distinctive here. People point to Bacon and Descartes, who are among the originators of modern thinking. But what is novel in them is connected more to new notions of the utility of theoretical reason and the link between mathematics and materialism than to a new sense of technology itself. People also point to the acquisitive individualism fostered by Hobbes and Locke and to its alliance with enlightened materialism and the support of novel inventions. But this too seems connected more to a new pace and degree of the old technology than to some radical break whereby technology becomes something deeply novel. The Green Revolution, however profound, is just farming by other means.

Perhaps what is distinctive belongs to the territory where difference in degree becomes difference in kind, so that with one more step we plunge headlong off a cliff into the existential abyss or across the border from West to East Berlin. The analogy, however, would still require us to say what distinguishes East from West and terra firma from a mad tumbling rush. What, after all, so differentiates a swift boat with many oarsmen from an airplane, a suspension bridge from logs thrown across a stream, or even the telephone from the marathon runner or pony express? All during the atomic age reasonable people could think of atom bombs merely as very big bombs we shouldn't drop rather than as heralds or instruments of some uncanny demon before whom we should tremble with an altogether novel shudder.

One might say next that modern technology produces something radically new not in this or that activity but by changing the context of many or all activities. The notion we discussed that the medium is the message is an instance of this view. Matters that need time to ripen lose that time in the swift rush of instant access by phone and computer. Natural rhythms are sped and slowed by drugs and other chemicals. Our scope of responsibility expands beyond home, neighborhood, and city to the entire environment, and to species themselves.

Even here, as we indicated earlier, one wonders if the change is as radical as it seems. When every action is broadcast immediately to a waiting world, politicians need to conduct themselves differently from when speeches were written on the backs of envelopes and read days later by a worried nation. But politicians have adapted well enough, and nothing earth-shatteringly new informs their judgment or behavior. More or less the same deals are consummated on cell phones as used to be through operators and before that in gentlemen's clubs. The largest differences one thinks of, in fact, have as much to do with the passing of such gentlemen in a democratic age as they do with the newer instruments of war and play. No doubt technology had something to do with such gentlemen's disappearance, but it was not the only or leading cause. In any event, have not the changes brought about by our technological instruments, at least until now, still been in step with the normal changes from generation to generation?

The third usual way to consider technology to be radically new is to argue that our first awareness of phenomena, their first presentation to us, has in some radical, general, and pervasive way been changed by technology. The outstanding version of this argument is the powerful statement of Martin Heidegger. Heidegger thinks that the essence of technology is that everything first approaches us as a standing reserve to be manipulated and transformed. One might think of how our natural objects become natural "resources" and how we see these resources as interchangeable instances of energy to be unlocked. Or, one might think of "human" resource departments that share space with the people in charge of office supplies.

The main point here is that we humans first see ourselves as standing reserve too. Our ends and goals, our environing space, the time spans of a lifetime, the occasions for effort and success, the elements of communication, all first come to light as fungible, interchangeable, stripped of their vital forms and differences. Nothing can be a guiding end, because nothing is first experienced as guiding and shaping. Nothing is experienced primarily as bringing matters to a stand and giving them direction within an appropriate place and time.

If this is true, the abiding power of health, love, knowledge, and courage that still seem to force our new mastery of distance and time along familiar paths is illusory or mostly illusory. Technology ultimately is not a powerful means or medium for familiar ends that are experienced largely as they have been always. It transforms our experience of ends, and it changes their significance and effect. Once the environment becomes a vast smokestack and mine, for example, any vital connection to its permanence, independence, or presence becomes lost. We see it as ours alone; we are in no way its. It is desecrated, and ways and lives dependent on communion (and appreciation) rather than intervention are threatened or destroyed. When we grasp the enveloping world only as interchangeable material or ignore it altogether, we necessarily distort the actions and choices that take place within it.

One obvious response to this situation is to do something about it. Environmentalism, concerns about the general effect of media, worries about global commodification—still another example of a "technologically" pervasive way or manner in which things are said first to meet or surround us—all contain ideas for reform. The reform often is radical or stems from a radical perspective, one that is general or global. Indeed, overall worries about the environment, media, and capitalist commodification are the source of unity in many anticapitalist and egalitarian movements. Today's anti-Americanism is largely envy of our power but it also is connected to dislike of the United States as the prime mover behind this new technological context of banality, physical degradation, and manipulation.

These views also are a source of notions that we must take aggressive, affirmative, international regulatory responsibility for the whole future because our actions affect the whole.[2] We are directly and publicly responsible for the future existence of man and the world, which we can destroy. If a god will not save us, then perhaps a properly green Belgian bureaucrat will. For Heidegger himself, however, notions that we might take control of technology and direct it are misplaced. The difficulty is that we will see our own responsibilities in an inevitably technological manner. Our attempt to control and use technology will be distorted by the way we approach ourselves and our ends as formless reserves and resources. Efforts to deal with the problem belong to and exacerbate it.[3]

DEALING WITH TECHNOLOGY PRACTICALLY

If we step back from these claims, we may make several additional points. One is that concrete concerns about global warming, population growth, fossil-fuel depletion, ozone holes, media conglomerates, or unnatural food usually replace (or stand for) these more totalizing conceptions I have just outlined.[4] As specific concerns, the worries are true or false, and indeed, many have proved to be false. The actual problems of the environment are dealt with by technology in the ordinary sense applied to particular issues of air, water, and resources. The pervasiveness of the media's flat immediacy is, as we have suggested, not so dominant a fact that economic competition, democratic politics, and thoughtful deliberation cannot affect it and create a situation that fifty years from now will look different from today's. Commodification and urbanization also are facts, but any honest appraisal recognizes that attachment to specific people, places, and things is genuinely and even eagerly sought, if in a new way.

So, the notion that we need a single-minded pervasive public attention to these technological issues or that otherwise we are doomed has for now proved untrue. We have not required the kind of general or world-controlling institutions some believe necessary to discharge a responsibility as broad as the supposed breadth of the technological problem. The view has turned out to be wrong that we need to face technology as a whole and that problems with huge effects (the bomb, say, or ozone) require a dominant world institution. The connected view that pervasive caution or risk aversion must be the attitude when the future of the species is in our hands also proves not quite right. Some public caution, some public and international agreements surrounded by responsible individual judgment and entrepreneurial action, seem for now to be more politically sensible and effective.

This suggests that the responsible approach to technology is generally one that does not conceive it as being in practice pervasively novel but, rather, attempts to foster responsibility within the context of free choice directed to sensible ends. The real issue is: How do we grasp free choice and sensible ends? I will consider this question in terms of biotechnology, where the issue is most pressing and profound.

TECHNOLOGY AND OUR ENDS

Let us return to the notion that what is radical in technology is its effect on the contexts of space and time, of distance and immediacy, of scope and size. We experience through the media massive, instant, fears and joys—everywhere, everyone, every instant. What, however, makes these experiences meaningful? What makes them hopes and joys? Are they not such in terms of our ordinary ends and desires? It is precisely for this reason, I would argue, that today's narrowing space and time and expanding powers of destruction are not, as such, so radical. The horror of a hundred thousand killed by a nuclear bomb takes its measure from the death of one who is beloved. Words of consolation broadcast to millions take their lead from words of consolation spoken softly to a few. The real issue, therefore, the true question of novelty, is whether technology changes or affects these ends themselves.

We may put the same point in the following way. The argument against technology, either directly or when the Heideggerian view of its uncanny pervasiveness turns into more concrete environmentalism or opposition to global media, trades on notions of what is good. Technology is a means or a stance that is said to harm. Harm what? What are the governing ends and goals that it perverts? A particular notion of careful deliberation and/or more equal access that mass media threaten; a view of the health, beauty, safety, and peace that environmental degradation or atomic weapons risk; a sense of the just rewards, dignity, and respect challenged by commodification—all these are thought to be threatened by technology. The wish to control technology responsibly or even radically restrict it has a purpose, and this purpose is to preserve these ends as we now understand (and dispute) them. So, the truly central task in dealing with technology responsibly is to know the ends we seek to enjoy, primarily as they struck us reasonably and commonsensically well before the advent of modern technology and its supposed radical novelty.[5]

What is new or newest in technology, I therefore believe, would need to be found in some deep effect it has on how we understand our goals and what is good about them and in our ability to experience them. This is why biotechnology is so important. Drugs that reduce aggression and pride inevitably will affect a whole range of human activities. Interventions into the brain with inadequate understanding of what makes good things good will have unpredictable results. The subtle links between action and thought, between spirit, desire, and reason, are so poorly understood that the effect of intervention can unintentionally be disastrous.

BIOTECHNOLOGY AND OUR UNDERSTANDING OF ENDS

To advance our topic I must now discuss generally what we mean by "good." What is good is satisfying, as in a good meal; complete, as in "Good" when a job is over; fitting, as with a good turn of phrase; beneficial, as with health or one's assets (one's "goods"); or useful, as with a good hammer. What is merely good can be better, but what is really, truly, or fully good or excellent apparently cannot. What is good, moreover, is pleasurable or enjoyable, as is a good piece of music; guiding, as is a good way out of a fix or into a town; or desirable, as is a good house for the house hunter or wine for the oenophile. What is good "works" and causes distress when lost.

These meanings are linked. What satisfies completes, if only briefly. What benefits belongs to what satisfies, as cold drink benefits a thirsty man, or is itself a source or instance of satisfaction, as is health. What is useful is used for completion. The guiding meaning of being good is to be satisfactory or complete, and the good things guide our actions by being instances of, or useful for, satisfaction or completion.[6]

What is best would satisfy most completely. This helps us understand how what is good is not "value neutral," as it might seem from this discussion. (For what if the satisfactory job is an assassination?) Much is satisfactory for a time but soon shows itself to be incomplete. Health can be everything when one is ill but hardly enough otherwise. Love cannot easily survive poverty or disappointment. The very satisfaction or completion that characterizes what is good carries with it almost always a continuing dissatisfaction or openness and often an easily reached surfeit or superfluity. What is best is most satisfying, most complete, although it seems that nothing that completes can complete simply or altogether.

Although there obviously is wide variety among useful and satisfying goods—food is not drink—we also should bring to sight the less visible variety in what we experience as, and mean by, completion. This variety is linked to the different types of universals or wholes; it is connected to the several ways in which reason can group and distinguish things. The last bill in a hundred completes the sum differently from the last note in a quartet or the next child in a family. The wholes of which they are parts differ, some being present all at once, others not, some composing by ordering and arranging, others simply by adding, some with parts that are identical to each other, others with parts that are unique, some with parts that are indispensable, others with parts that are expendable, and so on. This variety in the structure and organization of wholes is connected to how we experience good things as satisfying. Moderation (frugality) to increase wealth is not the same experience as the moderate (measured) enjoyment of pleasure. The satisfaction of hearing a beautiful harmony is not the same as the satisfaction of a full stomach; one can be ravishing or uplifting as the other is not. Human happiness is a completion or attempted completion of reason and feeling, and this means that it consists of satisfaction's structure as well as its content. Therefore, the intensity and complexity of reason and feeling vary as our understanding changes about how completion and satisfaction are composed.[7]

I emphasize reason, as I did when I discussed liberal education, because it is the element that distinguishes our experiences from that of animals and the inanimate. Emotions become human because they are invested with intellect. This endowment is visible not just because mind can control or direct them but because mind is implicit in their range, outreach, and complexity. The experience of music is not the experience of the senses alone or, clearly, of the intellect alone but of the senses elevated to the complexity and resonance of which mind is capable. The experience of love inevitably is structured even in the intensity of its simplicity by the subtle rational relationships involved in a union that enhances the individual and is directed toward a still more original singularity, a child. These intellectual complexities are not after-the-fact talk but of the essence of the experience itself.

What unwittingly (or wittingly) restricts or redirects the mind or neuters the passions that belong to motivating and using the mind will, therefore, diminish us. Enhancements to our powers need not be harmful, but putative enhancement may distort proper enjoyment and use.[8] For what counts as the excellence of our powers is not altogether (or, really, at all) at our disposal. What is (and must continue to be) at our disposal, however, and is therefore especially at risk, is actually to use them excellently. To employ actively any of our powers well, or even to explore the depth of what we enjoy passively (say, naturally beautiful objects), we require a subtle and complex combination of our reason and passions.

Because proper thought is independent from the physical (the three angles of a triangle equal 180 degrees, whatever happens in the brain) and because the experience of the passions involves thought, what we can and should seek to achieve biotechnically is limited.[9] Thought's connection to the passions, however, and the link between thinking and its material base are central reasons why bioengineering makes us worry. Spiritless men neither think nor enjoy.

Another reason some might worry about biotechnology's effect involves the world of the senses or passions more directly. The particular ways in which we sensually experience happiness are changing constantly. Generations record the comings and goings of types of art and music, for example, and of economic lives and political communities.

Here too, we should see that technology cannot alter certain limits in the relationship between experience and its external conditions or objects. There are only so many opportunities for political power, great wealth, and owning limited resources like homes on the California beach. Faithful love always will demand unswerving attention. Technology cannot change these limits, for they are inherent in these experiences themselves as they reach to what is outside us. The same factors that make impossible Marxist or other "utopias" also will make impossible any utopia that technology believes it can bring about. In governing technology we will need to guard against the distortions we produce when trying to implement the impossible.

The effects of technology if it advances (and does not inadvertently diminish) capacities, however, will likely be to change how we distribute inherently limited resources, for the proportions of those who deserve and those who possess will change. We will find ourselves with more of some things and less of others because of what the more beautiful or intelligent people biotechnology helps to create merit and think they merit. Although we could speculate plausibly about what is likely to happen, I am not certain that the actual shape of political and economic life will be radically different from what we see today.

One also might fear that the natural ways of birth and death are now so subject to manipulation that the experience of happiness grounded in these root facts will be distorted and that these changes will be more broad and less reversible than the scope and pace of the economic, artistic, and political changes that we have come to expect. Technology not only promises here—by, say, extending life—but threatens. What is at risk in biochemical manipulation is not just the effective range, depth, and extremes of passion and thought but also the particular beginning and conclusion that always have shaped vital human experiences. So, although learning and remembering what makes good things good is the most useful and important general standpoint from which to deal with technology, we also will need something that more directly and precisely affects us as individuals.

I wish to begin discussing this issue by turning again to responsibility. Technology is not as radical as some argue, but it surely forces or allows us to choose some of what we once took for granted. Indeed, much that we do now is voluntary—ties of religion, location, profession, and family are by historical standards remarkably optional. One way to approach technology properly, therefore, is to explore the meaning and proper direction of modern freedom. When we use freedom correctly, we have argued, we use it (or are said to use it) responsibly. Responsibility correctly understood should therefore be a clue for dealing well with what is new technologically. The issue is how goals and ends can increasingly be matters of choice while at the same time the true desirability of these ends and the conditions for experiencing them can be allowed to flourish. We must elevate both what we choose and our self-understanding as those who choose.

USING TECHNOLOGY RESPONSIBLY

The first task in using technology responsibly is not to harm responsible freedom itself. That is, the first task is to preserve responsible character. The second task is to elevate responsibility's use as much as possible so that the flattening of goods and experience to which it is prone does not dominate. Responsibility as a characteristic of far-sightedness for oneself, effectiveness for oneself and others, and breadth for those who take on public tasks does not guarantee on its own a full understanding of ends. It is too egalitarian and materialistic and too neutral toward the substance of happiness, even though it fosters qualities that enable each to pursue happiness successfully.

It seems to me that acting reasonably and responsibly in one's own sphere, a sphere that one sometimes extends publicly is, nonetheless, the best way to begin to enjoy technology's fruits while controlling its consequences. Such action involves exercising rights and freedoms and, therefore, the clash of our actions within freedom's general protection. Not global planning and blanket decisions but the adjustment that comes from the conflict of active, responsible, energies, including political enterprise and compromise, is the most useful practice. This competition calls on the widest use of human talent, does not rigidify narrow views, and preserves active freedom. Put another way, not this or that end but responsibly dealing with our ends is the first guideline in using technology. Character itself is a central goal.

This suggests that handling technology responsibly is largely (not completely) achieved by doing as we have all along. Contemporary technology's proper restraints and benefits are not altogether fixed. They change because of the continuing exercise of our freedom to discover and implement, and because regulatory regimes that first appear necessary are tightened and then loosened by responsible political officials. The regulatory guideline with technology is to consider the negative consequences that a responsible people wants to control, to see how to control them without controlling more than one wishes, and to adjust this bureaucratically. There ought to be some regulation of technology (because the consequences of using it can be dangerous and hard to reverse and because the possibilities for economic monopoly are ever present), but it ought to exist within a political atmosphere that we strive to make a responsible political atmosphere. This has proved successful so far in regulating but not overregulating the environment, patents, communications, atomic energy and so on. I would not presume to itemize the concrete restrictions the public requires today in these areas, but I would presume to say that public limits still need to be under political and not merely bureaucratic control; that they should reflect the usually continuing political battles about the issues they consider; and that private and public responsibility are themselves central goods to be preserved. We do not want overly to politicize central issues, but we do want to keep them politically in play.

TECHNOLOGY AND MORALITY

These same considerations—the freedom of political responsibility as both means and end of liberal democracy—largely should govern regulation of biotechnology. Indeed, were technologies such as cloning, stem-cell research, and genetic manipulation mostly identical to the usual pharmaceuticals, environmental impacts, or even weaponry, our recommendations would also largely be the same: some regulation is desirable but it should be grudging and minimal so that responsible freedom and private discovery are not hampered unduly. Regulatory regimes would control dangerous procedures (as we do with nuclear regulation) and also, perhaps, those with obviously harmful or risky effects on happiness and excellence. The result would be that the overall growth of biotechnical technique under the banner of health and security would continue.

Are there not some standards for regulation, however, that should have special weight in biotechnology? One example might be standards that sometimes outweigh calculations of benefit, moral standards, say, or equality of rights. Morally based controls on using technology sometimes are effective, and we already make them the ground for many legal prohibitions: we are rightly appalled by the "persuasion" or obfuscation that turns people into unwitting guinea pigs; we do not allow some to be forced to sacrifice organs for others. Merely moral limits are ineffective, however, if they too insistently contradict what is publicly and privately useful. Indeed, what is right and what is beneficial fit together better than we sometimes are taught: we prohibit murder and theft because punishing them makes civilized life possible, not just because they are wrong. In my judgment, it will and should also be difficult to regulate biotechnical advance simply on the grounds of moral claims divorced from obvious advantages. When (purported) moral or religious commands are split from such benefits as health they run the risk of being arbitrary and excessive. I therefore think that simply moral arguments or morally grounded regulations that go much beyond what already is illegal are unlikely to halt biotechnology's spread when countervailed by obvious advantages.

REVERENCE AND RESPONSIBILITY

I am arguing that we should guide choices to enhance our qualities technologically (and to intervene generally) through intelligent reflection on the conditions (especially of thought) under which we can experience what is good, a sound sense of our limits, and respect for the complexity of connections that we might upset inadvertently.

Such guidance also requires that we secure the grounds on which we think enough of ourselves to want to elevate ourselves and to use our powers effectively for what is best. Here, I believe, we might reasonably support regulation based on standards and concerns that go beyond obvious dangers and illegalities. For, regulation also is appropriate when what we might choose could distort the conditions under which we experience the (self)-understanding and pride that lead us to make the best of ourselves. One reason I am arguing that preserving liberal responsibility is a guide to using technology is that the self capable of free responsibility is the most general modern and secular instance of such dignity. Responsible freedom, however important, is only one such instance, and not sufficiently effective, because our current self-understanding is prone to the same mistakes of trivializing and flattening, as is our liberal understanding of goods generally. Indeed, the most significant such general conception is reverence or awe. Responsible freedom as opening to reverence, awe, or wonder (and the goals of our freedom as they open to ends in the light of such phenomena) is the natural standpoint from which to consider our own choices and limits. The wide general agreement to prohibit reproductive cloning is connected not only to its dangers for the cloned but also to a proper sense of our pride, or reverence for what deserves to be revered in us.

Reverence is the experience of the inviolability of what is unique, in its possibilities of excelling. It is not, as is sometimes said, only toward what is ineffably or mysteriously beyond but also for ourselves as oriented to what is best. Reverence is owed the things that perfect us and our own possibilities of choosing perfection, our own possibilities of virtue, of wisdom, courage, moderation, and justice. It therefore is oriented to our reason and freedom and, consequently, to what we share with others; it is an experience at the ground of respect for equality in rights and hence of responsible freedom. We treat most reverentially those for whom we have special or unique responsibility, the objects of our fullest devotion and love.

The experience of what deserves or occasions reverence is central in what is moral, in the things we do not do, places we do not defile, or people we do not mock—even, or especially, when these actions would bring us benefit. Without reverence there can be little true pride or love, and without pride or love, what good can our technology actually do? Who in their absence will seek to elevate himself or understand what excellence means? The experience of reverence is coeval with an experience of the goods that guide us. This is why some legal or regulatory limits to our actions that sacrilize this restraint by placing certain actions beyond the pale—in the realms of birth and death most obviously—are fundamental even if from the standpoint of calculating benefits they appear "irrational."

The experience of reverence, however, especially as it congeals into a system of rigid morality or religion, should not always direct behavior, precisely because what is useful, necessary, beneficial, or naturally satisfying is another guide, and because of the unique interests and responsibilities that inevitably bias and lead us. What is too distant from freedom, from what is useful, and from reasonable justification is arbitrary and, therefore, cannot succeed well. When the sacred is improperly developed in contradiction to the natural and, especially, the naturally excellent and naturally equal, it can settle on what is false or even dangerous. The twin of proper reverence is proper irreverence, which recognizes the gap between our aspirations and our achievements and, therefore, helps prevent the mistaken dogma that a "moral" or religious code or prohibition can completely replace an excellence for which we can only strive, or free us from the need for ordinary happiness and satisfaction. Genuine reverence, of course, is related to much of what properly is believed sacred, because it protects our ability to choose what is naturally, reasonably, high, and to think of ourselves as worthy of such choices and as required to make them.

I conclude that drawing some lines in using biotechnology is desirable even if a technique promises to advance health or enhance capacities, as long as drawing lines is not irresponsible, morally arbitrary, or imprudent. It would not be irresponsible whenever salutary alternatives to risky change can be found or arbitrary wherever restraint can reasonably be justified in terms of our proper pride. It would not be imprudent when the risks to the full and complex subtlety of our mind and passions are unknown, ill considered, or ignored. Restraint is especially important if we are to think enough of ourselves to direct properly the vast changes of which we are capable.

Prohibiting reproductive cloning and restricting the use of stem cells in the manner recently supported by President Bush follow in a relatively straightforward way from my discussion. So too, if less straightforwardly, does restricting the use of mind-altering pharmaceuticals to (reversible) therapy, rather than, as at present, employing them for "enhancement." Today's issues, however, will not be the only issues or today's capacities our only powers.

CONCLUSION

I will conclude by restating my major points. What is most radical in today's technology is not its origin in modern philosophy or even its pervasive effect on the way we see ourselves and our surroundings. These are of a piece with liberal democratic thought and politics generally. Liberal democracy favors some goods, such as health, more than others, such as nobility; promises to deliver a superfluity of these goods; and subtly affects our experience of good things so that these promises can be met. It does not, however, completely overturn our ordinary understanding of these goods or our experience of them.

Contemporary technology, however, is radical because it threatens to do just that. This threat is especially evident in biotechnology, because the subtle relations between thought and passions that define experience and its worth can be upset by our genetic and pharmaceutical interventions. We cannot change what makes good things good; this permanence centers for us on the independence of thought and the endowment of the passions with intellect. We can, however, change the degree and completeness of the spirit and intelligence with which we pursue what is good and the physical conditions on which these rely. In order to improve the chance that change will not be change for the worse, we need to reflect on the experience of what is good, and our reflections must now become more urgent than usual.

Reflection on our ends is insufficient, however, because we also must attend to the situation and character of liberty with which we make our public and private choices. The heart of this character is responsibility; we must learn or remember to use our freedom responsibly. This means to use it through and for a character anchored in habits that allow each of us to be effective for himself and others and to employ these qualities in wider and wider spheres. Preserving such responsibility is a standard for using technology properly. It is an insufficient standard, however, because the worth of responsible freedom is limited by the flat, equal, and voluntaristic way in which it approaches goods and satisfaction. It needs to be elevated to a more complete grasp of the link between thought and passions and the nature, true experience, and differing worth of good things. This elevation involves both educated reflection on what is good and a grasp of the ground of responsible freedom in reverence and even awe, for this grasp helps us see ourselves in such a way that we wish to make the best of ourselves. Natural reverence also requires experiences like those provided by its twin, irreverence, so that it does not become dogmatic, legalistic, self-satisfied, or too divorced from natural benefits.

Responsible freedom so elevated provides a standpoint from which to limit technological interventions that may seem beneficial but would cause us to lose sight of the excellence and inviolability of the human being for whom the benefit supposedly is sought. Reproductive and therapeutic cloning can now sensibly be banned whatever their immediate benefit. Benefit, however, is usually a reasonable standard when it can be achieved without violating the heart of human freedom and when it is understood properly. In this regard therapy is a more obvious good than "enhancement" until we understood more clearly what makes subtle goods worthwhile.

Regulation, I have just suggested, is not unreasonable. We should, however, carry it out in the spirit I have been sketching and through the broad mechanisms I have discussed: leeway for private effort and discovery, political control and transparency, and a spirit of rigorous and responsible competition both within government and outside it. As in other cases, we should develop international regulatory regimes only as matters of necessity, because free government and its spirit of enterprise cannot well survive the size and scope of international control.

NOTES

1. I will use the terms "bioethics" and "biotechnology" and their variants interchangeably. An interesting recent book on biotechnology more directly, especially the issues of genetics, is Gregory Stock, *Redesigning Humans* (New York: Houghton Mifflin, 2002). Good general books on the broad issues are Francis Fukuyama, *Our Posthuman Future* (New York: Farrar, Straus and Giroux, 2002), and Leon Kass, *Life, Liberty and the Defense of Dignity: The Challenge for Bioethics* (New York: Encounter Books, 2003). A spirited but believably sober and informative recent book on the related topics of robots and artificial intelligence is Rodney Brooks, *Flesh and Machines* (New York: Pantheon Books, 2002).

2. We see this more or less implied in Hans Jonas's *The Imperative of Responsibility* (Chicago: University of Chicago Press, 1984), a work influenced by this broad Heideggerian sense and influential in some of the standpoints I just discussed. Heidegger's argument can be found in his essay "The Question about Technology." This appears most accessibly in Martin Heidegger, *Basic Writings*, ed. David Farrell Krell, rev. and exp. ed. (New York: HarperCollins, 1993).

3. In a related vein, some might say that wild fears of globalization, media conglomerates, and environmental interference demonstrate in their flat destructive leveling and willful ignorance of specific circumstances the very problem of rootless excess they wish to condemn. Left-wing nihilism or fascism is still nihilism or fascism.

4. In gathering their political support, however, even those who worry about concrete technological issues often rely on these general fears. So, ozone holes and population bombs are said to be grounded in, or to result in, apocalyptic change.

5. I mention reason because the attack on technology sometimes has an atavistic ring, and the concern is given its complexity by the return in Nietzsche, Heidegger, and their followers to so-called simple traditions, or the imaginations of poets, or the immediately prephilosophical and prescientific world. These standpoints, however, threaten to give away what one most wishes to protect, our rational powers. Thinking through the link between our ends as they are rationally informed and their prereflective wellsprings does, however, belong to reinvigorating these goals, our free response to them, and the pleasures we gain from them. Genuine reflection on what makes our goals good and on the place of thought in enriching or even threatening these goods is a central task if we are to govern technology responsibly, especially given the emergence of biotechnology. Post-Heideggerian thought can contribute to this.

6. Consider Mark Blitz, *Plato's Republic* (Claremont, Calif.: Gould Center, Claremont McKenna College, 1999), 24–28.

7. Considering these phenomena carefully and precisely is one way, and for the problem before us an immediately relevant way, to unravel some of the questions grouped too generally under the important phenomenon of "consciousness" discussed by analytic philosophers and scientists who are influenced by them. The complexity of what is whole is also one reason why simple teleology is inadequate. At the same time, this complexity and the orientation of our powers to activities and possibilities that are outside of, and might satisfy, them suggest why confidence that we are unlikely to do away with human abilities, as we can list and describe them generally, is insufficient to guide us in using these powers well or to prevent us from constraining them inadvertently. Consider Jerry Weinberger, "What's at the Bottom of the Slippery Slope: A Post-Human Future?" *Perspectives on Political Science* (Spring 2003).

8. "Mind expanding" drugs show this.

9. Discussions of what to do with our biotechnical power are pointless unless we see that although there is a physical or chemical analogue to our thoughts and experiences, these experiences are not identical to the analogue. Whatever happens in the brain when we make a true deduction in Euclidean geometry, the truth of the deduction differs from what happens in the brain. Understanding or experiencing this truth must therefore also differ from what happens in the brain, and it is only because we know what this understanding means that we can look for the chemical activities that accompany or even in some sense cause it. Similarly, that murder is wrong and seeing that it is wrong are not equivalent to what

happens in the brain of someone who understands it is wrong. I also would argue that human passions and emotions are not identical to their analogous brain activity. Emotions are not emotional phenomena at all except insofar as they reach out to or have in mind conceptually a whole complex of possible objects of satisfaction and disappointment. Moreover, precisely because our passions can be discussed, controlled, and experienced in terms of reason, there are truths about them that are irreducible to a group of physical facts connected to them. One example I have in mind is Aristotle's connections, in his *Ethics,* among virtue, practical reason, and the passions. These points, if correct, are important because they indicate limits to what we can produce biochemically that do not arise from technical capacity but from the nature of what can be made. Science cannot turn vice into virtue or tyranny into just rule. It cannot equalize petty satisfaction and intense, uplifting, and encompassing love. That said, it is possible to flatten or excite the passions intentionally or inadvertently, precisely because they do have chemical analogues or a chemical base. Grand passion cannot be reduced to, but is not simply independent of, its underlying material. (The point I am making does not require that today's human beings be the only conscious, intelligent, or emotional beings. The point is that there are limits to what any such being can do, whatever the increases in intelligence, further shrinking of distances in space and time, or greater sensory powers we can give ourselves. Such change may, of course, have significant effects on how we live or give us new sources of happiness, which at the same time will mean that we will give up others.)

8

LOCKE'S DOCTRINE OF RESPONSIBLE ACTION

We cannot understand the limits and worth of liberal responsibility fully unless we grasp its theoretical ground more directly. For its power lies not only in the responsibility and practical institutions it fosters but also in their justification. Its limits, moreover, are not confined to our need to consider more broadly than liberalism what is good but also are visible in the way its perspective is justified. These issues should be clarified, and to do so I will turn now to a discussion of liberalism's most unified philosophical source, the work of John Locke.

I will try to show that the heart of Locke's understanding of responsible action, the heart of his liberalism, is a novel moral ontology. An understanding of the possibility of "good" accompanies his view that any particular thing or feeling is good. This understanding fits together with and guides the experiences of religious dogma, the self, knowledge, and liberty that direct Locke's articulation of these subjects.[1]

Because my goal here is to explore liberal responsibility's philosophical roots, I necessarily develop and discuss issues more theoretically than in previous chapters. I begin by showing how Locke seeks to replace religious dogma with natural common sense (thus advancing religious toleration) and go on to describe the central elements of and limits to this common sense. I then state my thesis concerning Locke's moral ontology, develop its connection to Locke's basic understanding of liberty—the immediate intellectual source of liberal responsibility—and conclude by linking Locke's justification of political authority and industriousness to this understanding. I bring out the root connection of Locke's argument and responsibility most directly in the chapter's final sections.[2]

LOCKE'S RHETORICAL STARTING POINT

Locke begins his major works—the *Essay Concerning Human Understanding* and the *Two Treatises of Government*—by dealing with the opinions that block our access to what he wishes to argue. This starting point is central to the success of liberalism. Locke thinks that we can know many things certainly, or highly probably, but that interests, group and party prejudices, words with unclear reference, habits, accidents, failed discoveries, and uncertainty come together to cause us to know less than we might. Our inadequacies are not permanent, however; the evidence is readily available on which to build true understanding of the most important matters.[3]

Central to achieving clear access to this evidence is to shake the reigning religious or scholastic dogmas. These are the opinions Locke is most concerned to clear away. Scholars' controversies about the precise status of Locke's belief should not blind us to the immense importance of this enlightenment at the root of liberalism. In the *Two Treatises,* Locke undermines what Scripture indicates about rule and authority or what he tells us others mistakenly believe Scripture to indicate. He then tries to put government on a natural base and reinterprets Scripture to conform to this base. In the *Essay* he begins with the opinions of scholastic thinkers about knowledge and the ways to attain it, views that among other things support particular religious dogmas.[4]

Locke's chief immediate enemy in the *Essay* is the traditional doctrine of innate ideas, his deeper ongoing enemy is the doctrine of essential substances, and the scholastic practice he most questions is disputatious word mongering. These unreasonable views and practices are caused by interest, mistaken judgments of probability, and failure to love truth. When errors do not stem from these they flow from faith itself. Indeed, religion that does not see its links to reason or believes itself not to improve reason but to supplant or ignore it is rooted in "enthusiasm." Against enthusiasm Locke argues unqualifiedly.[5]

THE *ESSAY'S* RHETORICAL GOALS

To clarify further Locke's attempt to separate theoretical investigation and political practice from religious dogma (and ideas connected to it), it will be useful to summarize what Locke says about God in the *Essay*.

The first point is that Locke does not adjust reason to Scripture, but the opposite. He nowhere decides against something reasonable because Scripture tells him otherwise, but interprets Scripture to conform to reason.[6] The second point is related: however much faith might answer more certainly questions that reason can answer only probably if at all, in Locke's discussion faith never dictates actions that reason does not dictate already. Just reward and punishment in an afterlife are not required for moral behavior to be choice-worthy on earth. Our theoretical inquiries do not rely upon choosing some direction that only faith can set. In general, no intelligible statement or directive of faith can dispense with reason or fail to indicate (even if inadvertently) the superiority of the love of truth to other arts and the superiority of reason as the instrument or expression of this love. Indeed, an omnipotent yet unreasonably willful god would hardly differ from a tyrant.[7]

Keeping these central points in mind we can now examine several specific arguments. Locke believes we can prove that God exists, that however unknowable God's concrete powers, we can grasp His existence and the general outline of His powers reasonably well.[8] Because everything has a cause and the immaterial, or at least thought, cannot arise from the material, some thinking being must have existed eternally. We know it is not we. We also know that all spiritual or intellectual power must come from this eternal cause, for it could come from nowhere else. An eternal omnipotent power therefore exists, and Locke further claims that because He must have made other beings His omniscience and providence also have been established.

These arguments are or seem weak in several respects. Even if true they do not demonstrate that there is one god rather than many. (Locke claims to believe that there could be any number of thinking sensible beings—angels, say—with powers greater than our own. Could there not be many gods sufficiently powerful to create or form everything material and immaterial?) God's omnipotence is demonstrated only to the extent that, say, the first stone rolling down a hill causes an avalanche. The avalanche's power is not all in the stone, nor could the stone reverse the avalanche's effects. Providence and omniscience are not argued for at all. Moreover, Locke's view that the immaterial cannot arise from the material is perhaps plausible but hardly dispositive. The differences or gaps between seeing red, thinking "red," choosing to reach for a red flower, and the bodily motions associated with these actions do not suffice to show that the "spiritual" action could not have arisen from material causes, however different the spiritual and material are in their meaning and quality once spiritual, reasonable, or free action does begin to exist.[9]

Did Locke see these weaknesses and ignore them for his political or rhetorical purposes, or was he persuaded by his arguments? It would be rash to claim the first, because the "weaknesses" of his argument may reflect not his but my own or any other challenger's mistakes. It also would be rash to claim that Locke fully convinced himself by his own arguments, however, because some—the brief mention of providence, say—are visibly weak or nonexistent. Perhaps the safest conclusion is this: Locke's limited claims are not necessary for or the ground of his practical conclusions, nor would they mislead, limit, or unalterably distort theoretical inquiry.[10]

Locke considers other relevant issues from the perspective of his basic points. Whatever God reveals beyond reason He reveals positively—by direct admonition, inspiration, or through Scripture. How could one know one is hearing the truth from God and not something fraudulent or the fevered concoction of one's own hopes, fears, pride, and intellectual laziness? For Locke, such inspired messages must be intelligible to our understanding and the evidence of their authorship must stand the usual evidentiary tests. Locke tells us why no serious person would doubt Caesar's existence, but he implicitly shows how the evidence could be less certain for any of Caesar's acts. In any event, nothing that we hear from others can be certain, however likely it is. Locke does not give a convincing reason beyond his own sometimes noble efforts to show that Scripture is reasonable why we should believe others who call it the word of God.[11] Indeed, his discussion of assent, faith, and error is conducted in fully secular terms.

The best direct evidence of a divinity who works beyond but not contrary to natural effects are miracles. Locke discusses them briefly in the *Essay*.[12] He gives (in other contexts in the *Essay*) good reason to doubt others' reports of miracles; we trust another's account that, say, some region has a permanently frozen lake because we have seen frozen lakes ourselves and can extrapolate. Trust depends on similarity in experience. A Caribbean king who had never seen ice, however, would find such a story incredible. We ourselves listen with skeptical amusement to stories of talking parrots who actually can reason and to Locke's third-hand reports of them. Locke implicitly suggests that tales of miracles have this same value.

Miracles we experience for ourselves suffer from similar difficulties. Would the Caribbean king seeing the frozen lake believe his eyes? If he believed his eyes would he not think the event miraculous? If he thought the "miracles" could in principle be explained reasonably, however, would he not sooner or later learn about natural ice? Locke believes (or pretends to believe) it possible that other rational beings exist whose rational and/or sensual capacities outstrip our own—that is, that human limits are not equivalent to the limits of reason's understanding. Assume, however, that humans alone can understand. Even then there is no way to know that an unusual event could not be traced to natural causes that we happen not to see or be able to see (now). Indeed, it is improbable that we could not so trace it, especially because we and Locke already know a rational being with sensual powers beyond those humans immediately enjoy, namely, ourselves with our microscopic and telescopic eyes and the sensory enhancements we have since developed. These powers become means better to discover nature and account for what otherwise might seem miraculous or merely random. So, not just others' reports of miracles but what look to be miracles one experiences oneself lack evidence of being miraculous, although Locke does not deny their possibility. The unusual impact of strange events, moreover, which seems to credit their being miraculous, may from a rational standpoint suggest especially good grounds to doubt that they are miraculous at all. An eclipse that is a miracle for some may for an inquiring mind be an outstanding clue to how nature works.[13]

In short, then, Locke himself never supports practical or theoretical actions that he cannot defend reasonably, and he leads us to doubt the credibility of what purport to be miracles and messages heard directly from God. This enables him to interpret Scripture so that it conforms to reason and sets the stage for Locke's replacing piety with toleration as the central virtue dealing with the public place of religion.[14]

LOCKE'S COMMON SENSE

Locke's success in clearing away religious underbrush and what grows or festers in it (in the *Essay* the doctrine of innate ideas) opens the way for a newly powerful yet permanently possible kind of common sense, namely, rational common sense. Locke does not elbow dogma aside only to allow rickety and uncertain arguments to replace it. Rather, he means to replace it more permanently with a rational ground that is easier to notice and harder to doubt. Locke believes that the evidence is readily available to support his views. Noticing and gathering it require no special training or equipment. All one need do is to look directly with and at one's own understanding, in immediate and only occasionally difficult ways. Men of affairs reason well enough, even if no professor has ever harangued them about the syllogism.[15]

Locke's argument is rationally commonsensical, therefore, because once he clears away the result of religious dogma he asks sensibly open-minded individuals to apply abilities they already have to follow arguments that are not stated technically and to use evidence always at their fingertips to check and validate these arguments. He replaces the authority and seeming inevitability of religious and socially constructed horizons as much as is possible with the most commonsensical and immediately accessible natural standpoint.[16] No religious dogma can be more evident than our natural beginning nor intelligibly conflict with it.[17]

THE BASIC ELEMENTS OF LOCKE'S THOUGHT

Let us now begin to discuss the elements of Locke's common sense. Their power derives from the fact that they are independent and easily visible. As one might say classically, the elements of Locke's common sense are the things in nature that are, or look unchallengeably to be, first for each of us. The primary and most basic elements must be both simple and evident, for what is simple and evident are the matters that cannot be doubted, overcome, or avoided.

The basic elements in Locke prove always to be separated or isolated individuals. Compounds either are constructed altogether or are regular associations that we happen to notice among separate ideas. (Their association even may have a deep cause, but this we can hardly know.) We build our understanding from separate ideas that we grasp through our senses and by reflecting on the actions of our mind, actions largely (or perhaps exclusively) occasioned by dealing with sensory ideas. Everything that we do not sense directly or observe in ourselves is made up or put together and is not found in nature beyond our construction and its elements. Certain, very few, basic qualities inhere in things themselves—extension, solidity, figure, motion, and number: these in turn cause us to sense secondary qualities such as color.[18] Locke is less clear whether mental actions—thought, memory, doubt, etc.—are themselves (all) primary or (some) merely the way the primary processes affect us when we look at ourselves looking at them. In any event, the inner essence both of bodies ("matter") and understanding ("spirit") is beyond our comprehension, if it exists at all.

The questions we might raise about this notion of simplicity should not detract from the immediate clarity of what Locke says. It is the first or very much among the first points that come to mind once we reflect on our actions. This is so because a simple idea is what is most beyond dispute. Many now say that we see first not ideas but things, cows, not brown and white breathing bodies that make a distinctive sound, have a distinctive figure, regularly give milk, and so on. Locke, however, does not believe that we see such things first of all— and this is all the more true for, say, "just" things—for several reasons. The more complex an idea the more difficult to say it is known by us all originally, known by the true "naturals," such as children.[19] Moreover, the properties that make up a supposedly real substance, say, gold, do not belong to it essentially but vary with our sophistication: to yellow we add hard, to both we add soluble in aqua regia, etc. The things we think we see are stable only if they answer to our definition. Furthermore, many things that we believe to be are mere fantasies and chimeras.

What never is fantastic and chimerical, however, are the ideas we understand through sense or self-reflection. They are the evidence to which we point when we discuss things. So, at the very least, Locke's appeal is to the evidence to which we must appeal once we begin to reflect: whether we actually see separate ideas first of all, they are the firm ground we do not make, the firm nature that is most obviously visible to us. One's own sense of what one sees and thinks and one's own understanding of free action according to preference are the only terra firma. Far from reflecting some arbitrary methodological individualism or atomism (and rather than appearing powerful to us only because it has shaped us), Locke's understanding of what counts as the clearest natural ground—individuals seeing ideas and the root of happiness in the ideas of pleasure and pain—is true, or at least naturally beguiling.

SOME APPARENT LIMITS TO
LOCKE'S COMMON SENSE

It is, however, not the whole truth. Locke's common sense appears to explore insufficiently the following question: what connects our ideas? This is an especially difficult issue because he is quite concerned to deny that there are substrata in which matters are connected (or if there are we cannot know much about them). In Locke the "what is" question does not point upward or universally to disputable essences but outward to a variety of qualities and downward to those qualities in their separateness. Actions and powers are more important and revealing than are supposedly unchanging forms.

Locke's basic answer to the question of unity is the following. There are no spiritual or material substrates, or we have no useful access to them. Nonetheless, I do have my own identity in my reflection on my will, my power of rational suspension, and my memory and consciousness as mine of activities and passive reception. This self-consciousness together with the unity of "I" as directly seen in my will provides one link among my various ideas.[20] Similarly, all sensible ideas go back to bodies. A body is a cohesion of solid, separable parts. It is (consequently) also countable and shaped. Shaped, countable, extended bodies are by the nature of these very ideas distinguished from each other.[21]

Locke makes other points relevant to the question of the connection of ideas, more indications than arguments that he fully works through.[22] Ideas are independent, and yet some are necessary for each other. There is no color without light and no light that is not an effect of the sun. Ideas do not show their full power in each circumstance, moreover, but display different powers in different circumstances, as a plant or chemical proves to cure a disease only when one tries it, having faced the disease in the first place. Everything in Euclid is contained in triangles, but this knowledge is not easily available.

So, although Locke does not clarify thematically the variety of connections that combine elements, the types of attraction that bring parts into a whole, or how we see and know them, he does see ideas as coming together in bodies or in "me" through addition, accretion, accident, and the necessity of means and environment.

Again, it is important to see how sensible Locke's view is, whatever its limits. For, if we look from the first natural perspective, is this not what we would say, namely, that on reflection things are compounds of various ideas or perceptions only some of which are in the things? That these ideas often rely on other ideas to be present or be noticed? That in different circumstances or "experiments" we learn more and more about their powers? And that individual things are prior to universals?

LOCKE'S MORAL ONTOLOGY

We are arguing that Locke intends to combat scholasticism with a more obvious natural ground for what is not questionable (namely, simple ideas) and that for him the basic instance of unity is the consciousness that accompanies each of our own perceptions and reflections, and each use of our powers.

Locke also employs a particular sense of cause and effect: causes make things happen. They are efficient causes.[23] The notion that another meaning of cause exists whereby a spiritual or material essence grounds all the elements of "gold" or "human" is one of Locke's objections to the theory of the existence of such substances.[24]

The importance of simple ideas, unity seen basically as identity of the self, causality understood as efficient, reason grasped as "abstraction," as putting particulars together and taking them apart (and therefore as seeing likenesses and generalities only after particulars), and (as we will see shortly) human liberty viewed as suspension and consideration before effecting—all these fit together. In what way?

Locke's intellectual goal is to release us from dogmatic scholasticism. It also is one of his religious and political goals. As an intellectual goal such releasing allows, although it does not guarantee, increased human knowledge. As a political goal it allows increased satisfaction of freedom and desire. As a religious goal it allows religion to be rationalized.

Locke projects these purposes—increased useful knowledge, freedom, satisfaction, and rational faith—ahead of his claims about human understanding and what justifies political authority. As Locke says, our powers of knowledge and capacity for language are fitted to use or to our "concernments."[25] These purposes are the ground of Locke's view of reason, causality, simplicity, and the self.

But how could Locke justify this apparent subordination of truth to his concerns? How could such subordination be anything but arbitrary, and if it is only arbitrary how could his arguments about understanding and authority be rational and free? One answer is that Locke believes his purposes can be justified. Therefore, the means that help to bring them about are justified. If utility were the only consideration, however, the doctrine of simple ideas and its related concepts could be full or partial lies as long as they were serviceable. They would not be lies, however, if Locke's understanding of what is good and of our leading purposes directs and coheres with his view of reason, causality, liberty, and the self not arbitrarily or partially but so that the elements are fully coordinated and equally intelligible.

The chief element of coordination is that the meaning, experience, and possibility of "good" that precede or accompany Locke's view that this or that is a good fit together with the meaning, experience, and possibility of the self, knowledge, and liberty. Pleasure and pain, for example, "are," and are causally effective, as simple ideas. This coordination is "ontological": the heart of Locke is a certain ontology of what is good and its fit with how we know what we know and how we ourselves are.[26] The meaning and possibility of knowledge flow from the meaning and experience of what can be good. All knowledge ultimately is practical—that is, it is gathered and exists in a way that can make it useful (although indifference to immediate utility is crucial to its final utility). Locke's particular goals, however—say, replacing dogmatic scholasticism with rational religion—do not force a view of knowledge that is merely a means to these ends but cannot otherwise be justified in his own terms, or according to the evidence. Rather, the experience of what is good that grounds the desirability of the goals fits with and shapes a correlative experience and understanding of knowledge and the self. The clarity of this understanding in turn strengthens Locke's articulation of our experience of what is good.

PLEASURE AND PAIN

To grasp better the central elements here (and how they are coordinated) I begin by looking at pleasure and pain. As I said, Locke believes that the ideas we construct and even many we simply notice and differentiate are governed by utility. We make and see what we can use. The goal of our use is pleasure, and avoiding pain. The horizon of pleasure and pain is the first and most vibrant one in terms of which other ideas stand out.

   Pleasure and pain are simple ideas. They also are natural in the sense we discussed earlier: we do not make them (they are spontaneous and original), and they always cover us all.[27] They are "original" in that they are present from the start; from the beginning, pleasure directs our actions and helps differentiate what we see into separate ideas (the many shades of red, say, that we connect to different fruit). Locke understands pleasure to be always effective, moreover, and it causes action not as a distant end but because it literally effects or causes our action from the start, and in this sense all the time. It does not move us by being something we must understand subtly but, literally, as something we feel or perceive. Pleasure also is always effective in the sense that it moves naturals, infants as well as adults. Pleasure and pain are simple ideas that are present and effectively impel us from the beginning.[28]

That pleasure and pain always are pushing us along effectively is less obvious than Locke makes it look. Pleasure seems often to be a goal that we imagine or remember, even vividly imagine or remember, but do not always enjoy. Moreover, it sometimes moves us by being desired, not merely felt, and desire, we would think, is yearning, not only or usually irritation. Yearning, in turn, is more or less complex or expansive as our soul and its objects are more or less expansive.

To understand desire as yearning, however, places in the driver's seat the variable and fleeting end, goal, or object rather than universally effective pleasure. Ends that differ among human beings would become the chief motives of our actions. If we are to understand desire as a steady, universal, unquestioned motivation linked to the mechanical operation of bodies, however, we must discover a more neutral and effective quality than yearning. Locke therefore thinks of desire as uneasiness, just as pain is uneasiness.[29] Unease is a way to grasp the sensation and movement of desire as it pushes or impels us, without needing to ground desire in its object. Pleasures as accretions of what is similar or identical are easier to grasp as what relieves or stops unease than as varying fulfillments. Satisfaction in Locke is reduced to the continual motion of unease and equilibrium, with no substantive ranking of pleasures and no attempt to connect the different types of pleasures and unease to different human powers.[30]

Locke does not limit uneasiness to desire. The other passions also move us by causing or being instances of unease. When one perceives, senses, or reflects on a passion, one is perceiving a mode of unease. Naturally, if all unease is identical, the passions would be identical. What accounts for their differences? Locke connects these differences to different things or durations as they thwart, aid, or define the approach of unease and its relief. The flat road to composure or equilibrium is interrupted by various bumps that cause unease, around which we move in different ways.[31]

It should be apparent from this account that for Locke truly to explore our human understanding he should explore his notion of pleasure more capaciously. He does not do this. He does not consider the varieties of satisfaction, enjoyment, and equilibrium, the precise connections between unease and what stops it, and the different kinds of complex motions that characterize our different passions. A certain notion of "end" (stoppage, equilibrium, composure) and of "good" (what brings this about) dominates, and it is coordinated with seeing pleasures in an equal and summative manner. Locke does not explore what he calls the delight, or sometimes the "relish," in pleasure as if it might go beyond relief; he treats it as the correlative of desire as uneasiness, not of desire as yearning, openness, or incompletion.[32] This limitation is connected to the truncated view of connection (of wholes and parts) and causality I mentioned earlier. There is a notion of the being and experience of satisfaction that, largely unexplored, is the perspective from which Locke understands the ideas of pleasure and pain that govern our action.

Although this perspective is largely unexplored, however, we should see that it, or at least these ideas, are commonsensical in the sense that on reflection we all can notice the dominance of pleasure, observe the variety of things that give us and others pleasure, and see that whatever else pleasure might be it is what stops or relieves irritation.[33] Is not Locke's view the first thing that comes to mind when a cold eye is turned inward to consider the meaning and dominance of pleasure and the actual effectiveness of the necessities—sleep, food, drink, even sex—that are met as necessities? Does not everything that moves us, from selfish grabbing of the final morsel on the frozen tundra to selfless sacrifice for others' comfort, need to move us as unease?[34]

FREEDOM

I am arguing that Locke's understanding of the meaning, experience, and possibility of pleasure is coordinate with (and central to) the meaning and possibility of the other ideas that come to light when he examines and discusses knowledge, the status of religion, the self, and the purposes of politics. Let us now discuss freedom, which for him is the root of political authority.

Locke connects freedom to power. The ability to make a change is active power; the ability to receive it is passive power. The best idea of active power is the idea of beginning a motion. We have this idea from reflection on ourselves, where we find that barely by willing it, barely by a thought of the mind, we can move the parts of our bodies which were at rest before.[35] The mind is made up of a number of powers, among them will. "That which we call the will," is "the power which the mind has . . . to order the consideration of any idea or the forbearing to consider it or to prefer the motion of any part of the body to its rest, and vice versa, in any particular instance."[36] To will is not precisely to prefer, however; we can prefer to fly rather than to walk, but no one wills it—volition comprehends only areas where man has dominion. So, the word will refers strictly to "the power of the mind to determine its thought, to the producing, continuing or stopping any action, as far as it depends on us"[37]

Freedom is related but not identical to this. A man is free when he has power to move or not move, think or not think, according to the determination of the will; freedom refers to our power to either do or not do something according to our will. Doing something voluntarily means doing it because we will it, even though we sometimes may not be doing it freely, in that we could not forbear from it even if we so desired. Any free action, then, must necessarily be willed and be voluntary; but an action may be done voluntarily without being done freely.

Freedom relates to action generally, to the mind's thoughts as well as the body's motions; we are free whenever we have the power to take up or drop a thought according to the will's determination. We necessarily have some thoughts, but whether to consider this thought or that often is our choice, though not always—for example, under torture. So, we are not free if there is "no choice, no volition" at all or if we lack the power to act or forbear to act according to our thought. A lack of freedom takes the form of compulsion or restraint; it would seem, then, that an increase in freedom can be attained only by an increase in dominion.

Given these analyses, the question of whether the will is free does not make sense for Locke because liberty and the will both are powers; neither is a subject. Locke argues that the real question is this: "What moves the mind, in every particular instance, to determine its general power of directing to this or that particular motion or rest?" The answer is uneasiness. "The motive for continuing in the same state or action, is only the present satisfaction in it; the motive to change is always some uneasiness." Indeed, it is the "greater uneasiness" that determines the will; whenever a greater uneasiness occurs the will is "determined to some new action, and the present delight neglected."[38]

The greatest present uneasiness, however, does not necessarily determine our will. Experience shows that the mind "has a power to suspend the execution and satisfaction of any of its desires, and so all, one after another." It "is at liberty to consider the objects of them, examine them at all sides, and weigh them with others. In this lies the liberty man has and from the not using of it right comes all that variety of mistakes, errors and faults which we run into in our endeavors after happiness." One might say that true liberty requires this power of suspension and the subsequent (or cotemporal) examining and considering. "During the *suspension* of any desire, before the *will* be determined to action . . . we have the opportunity to examine, view and judge of the good and evil of what we are going to do."[39] Moreover, it is possible for us to raise in ourselves a desire for something that we had not desired previously. An absent good will not be part of our misery until "due and repeated contemplation has brought it nearer to our minds, given some relish of it, and raised in us some desire: which then beginning to make a part of our present uneasiness, stands upon fair terms with the rest to be satisfied."[40] Desires, then, can be fostered, and the choice of which desire to follow is not determined immediately by which uneasiness is strongest; we sometimes can suspend a desire's fulfillment, judge the degree of good or evil its fulfillment could bring, and then determine our will by "the last judgment of good and evil." The will can usually be held undetermined until we have the "knowledge of the good and evil of what we desire."[41]

Locke is reticent about how far or near our natural gaze and therefore our calculation of good and evil should stretch—one day or one year?—and about how much we are considering ways and means to relieve our own present unease and how much we are worrying about wider concerns (or immediate consequences) for family, friends, and country. But he is clear that the core of liberty is examining our desires and their objects while we are suspending our satisfaction, and only then determining our preferences. Suspension so that for the moment all can be considered and treated indifferently is necessary for liberty.

Liberty as suspension and examination is coordinated with pleasure understood as eliminating unease. The suspension and consideration have their meaning as a waiting for or calculation of relief from unease and as an extension of this concern. They are not experienced in relation to pleasure otherwise conceived: liberty is not experienced as, say, a gathering for ebullience, overflow, energy, rule, or playful delight. Pleasure and what is good as the effective relief (stopping) of unease, and liberty as our suspending satisfaction and examining matters before determining our preferences are the core of responsibility, the ability to be effective when so much is open to so many, and to ourselves.

JUSTIFYING HUMAN FREEDOM

The greatest ease might seem to require that we dwell within the fullest suspension or indifference, never making a choice. Some unease exists, however, as long as preservation is not guaranteed automatically. The result of trying to remain utterly indifferent, therefore, would be buffeting by immediately importunate forces or desires and by random or conventional thoughts. The attempt to remain utterly suspended would result not in ease but in inaction and thoughtlessness, for considered unease leads to industry in order to relieve it. Once we judge that we have done all we "can or ought to do in pursuit of our happiness," then it is a "perfection of our nature" that we actually will and act in accordance with what we have determined.[42] The fullest satisfaction and liberty are not (the illusion of) unmediated suspension, but suspension and examination *for* the greatest possible relief from unease. Indeed, there are deep or lasting types of unease that Locke wishes not just to relieve but to cultivate: desire to produce, desire to know the ways and means to satisfy our desires generally, and desire to know the consequences of our satisfactions.[43] His goal is the maximum degree of productive thought and action. True liberty and happiness require not only suspension but also enlightenment, an outlook broad enough that narrow religious or other conventional views do not dominate. Freedom is allied to suspension that allows rational calculation to direct preferences and that therefore requires preferences to come to light as instances of unease that are amenable to rational control.[44]

We may still question, however, why equilibrium alone—conscious dreamless sleep (reverie, as it were)—would not be sufficient for happiness if somehow possible. Locke believes that active power is effecting, changing, or acting upon others or material bodies. Voluntary action and attaining pleasure require that we transform material into property and accumulate it actively. Locke intends that we human beings unleash our power and uncover our capacities for rational consideration, free action, and propertied transformation.[45] The qualities we can discover about things become available only when we redirect ourselves to learning and accumulating, and discover new natural powers. Indeed, what is new is noticed primarily or only when we use things as our own. This is to say that we must transform ourselves, coolly directing our preferences to useful industry, spurred by unease, discovering what nature makes available for our workmanship, above all seeing ourselves primarily as free selves. In this sense Locke's goal, concern with what in the *Second Treatise* he calls others' preservation (not just our own), involves conquering more and more unease rather than simply relieving one's own (temporary) unease or achieving mere equilibrium. Locke's goal for each of us is the ongoing movement from composure to discomfort to composure.[46] The effective self who is able to direct and expand both this movement and the powers that enable it to occur, what later (and throughout this book) we call the responsible self, is Locke's goal, more than the stable accretion of delights themselves. This self (and its freedom and unity) is not present or intelligible apart from unease and the possibilities of satisfaction that allow unease and relief to be experienced as such.

What justifies Locke's goal of the responsible, or effective, human being? We can justify his goal reasonably only in terms of our freedom, our reason, and our capacities. How, rationally, could we step outside these phenomena further to direct or justify them, or fail to employ them in that very effort? Locke justifies in precisely this way—our freedom is set loose and increases, our reason becomes more powerful and effective, our capacities are reformulated, rediscovered, and expanded. Conscious reverie does none of this, even were we able to attain it for a lifetime, as we are not, or in an afterlife.[47] As we have argued, moreover, Locke's understanding of these qualities is coherent. Freedom, reason, and desire all are of a piece, dealing with or being constituted by simple ideas and making, producing, being struck, and being satisfied by new qualities as a result. Increase, power, effectiveness, and expansion all are connected to the meaning of unease and to the possibility of thinking about how to deal with it. Locke does not choose a purpose that is ontologically incoherent with his grasp of choice, reason, and what is good, but, rather, develops what is inherent in the meaning, experience and possibility of these phenomena, as he sees them. This is the consistency at the core of Locke's work, and it explains how this or that aspect—the epistemology of simple ideas, natural enlightenment from religious darkness, pleasure, liberty or rights, the effective, responsible self—can in different circumstances appear to be his central thought or purpose. We may and must question the depth and range of Locke's understanding of these central qualities, but it would be untrue to claim that Locke inconsistently imports or relies upon old beliefs, beyond the degree to which he thinks that they are true.

Although Locke's arguments rest on common sense, on evidence that is readily available almost to all, caring directly for others, for "mankind's" preservation, belongs to the outsized responsibility of those few who take the long view, such as Locke himself. These are the ones whom Locke in the *Second Treatise* calls the industrious and rational. Their constant unease in the face of ignorance is needed to attain humanity's relief from unease generally. How, then, can their outsized actions actually be made useful beyond themselves, and how can they be defended? Given our claim concerning Locke's doubts about dogma, miracles, Scripture, and what for him are related theoretical concepts such as innate ideas, and given his attempt to replace the immediate authority of Scripture with the natural authority of the individual, it is consistent to suggest that Locke's politics are meant to protect us all from the defenders of dogma and to protect industrious investigators from scholasticism. He accomplishes this goal by grounding government on individual rather than paternal or religious authority, by making what we owe others a matter of just and effective political law rather than unexecuted and ineffective natural law, by tutoring our character in a responsible rather than obedient direction, by rationalizing (i.e., Lockeanizing) religion, and by allowing philosophy to become useful science.[48]

POLITICS: THE LIBERAL GROUND OF AUTHORITY

We see from Locke's *Two Treatises of Government* that the central goals of his politics are to protect rights and to protect property. We are equal in our rights.[49] In Locke's developed argument an individual right is the authority to determine one's preferences and the means to do so. Others can prevent my acting according to my will, but none can prevent my being determined by my preferences and in time by my considered preferences.[50] This liberty of judgment and voluntarism is the unalienable ground of our other freedoms. In this we are equal to each other. As is true of other substances such as gold, "man" is composed from many ideas. From among these ideas Locke chooses to ground government on one directly relevant to it—authority, or rightful effecting—and it is in this that we are equal.[51] He does not make up or invent what is not there; he chooses a feature that is natural and visibly significant once we turn to look at ourselves. For his full analysis of this idea, however, we must go beyond the *Two Treatises* to the *Essay*.

This trait or feature, although relevant to rule, is not the only one Locke could have selected on which to rest government, even naturally. Reason or understanding would be another possibility, given Locke's view of the ideas that comprise us. Still another would be the combined "man," the free action of our body or the combination of our freedom, reasoning, and body. Locke makes this totality the basis of what succeeds the first grounding in equal liberty; it becomes the heart of his notion of property. Property is the embodiment of free, voluntary, action, of power that serves our preferences. Property is the outside, as it were, of our natural inner independence. Property places "me," my person, outside into the material; it transforms what is other into a product or even an image of my preferences and (Locke especially hopes) my reasoned or industrious—my responsible—will. But we are much less evidently equal in this totality or even in our bodily similarity than we are in the liberty of scrutinizing our desires and their objects and being determined by our own unease. (This totality, furthermore, also is less distinct as an idea.) We also are more evidently equal in this liberty than in our degree of reasonable foresight.[52] Liberty to choose and be determined by preferences, to submit to and extend unease, is the only unalienable and equal ground of political authority.

One might still ask beyond this how Locke justifies the selection of liberty as the ground for authority, for even if it is the idea most central to rule, it yet might be incoherent with the central causes of knowledge and action. It would then ultimately (or proximally) prove contradictory or impossible. As I indicated earlier, however, Locke's choice is of a piece with the simplicity and clarity of other basic ideas, because liberty is the simplest and most evident natural ground of authority; with what is good, seen as naturally independent relief from unease (or "pleasure") and the means to this; and with the conception or projection of satisfaction, reason, and causality that are correlative with these ideas. Locke's root concepts are coherent.

Liberty and equality are coordinated at the ground of Locke's political thought, because we are equal in our liberty. This indicates that our liberty is most fundamental, for without it Locke could not defend our equality. Moreover, to suggest that equality is prior would be to suggest that equality as such rather than advancing pleasure, releasing us from religious tutelage, and discovering truths about nature (self-government in the widest sense), are Locke's goals. These other purposes, however, are more fundamental for the reasons I have given; they more substantively explicate, effect, and express the connected realm of ideas Locke explores, his actual notion of human action and its goals, and the tutelage he wishes to overcome. Mere equality—slavish equality—is more easily and otherwise achieved.[53]

Locke is more concerned to harness inequality in politics than to eliminate it. Economic and scientific inequality are not inequality in rights. By promoting equal rights, turning spirit to industry, conceiving thought as the labor of science, and limiting government's purpose, he tries to foster useful inequalities that do not challenge the root natural equality and independence of human beings. He therefore sets in motion the growth of responsibility—of responsible character and the institutions that work well with it—that has been our theme. Such responsibility is a common virtue of effectiveness that also allows, encourages, and exemplifies outsized success within the liberty we share equally. Responsibility and its correlated institutions have proved able to maintain a good order. We wonder, nonetheless, whether a Lockean revolution can be instigated or refreshed by anything short of extreme ambition and political virtue.

CONCLUSION

This chapter on Locke finishes my book on responsibility. It also could have begun it, in slightly different form. Perhaps this circle shows that a true conclusion is unnecessary or even impossible. In any event, no purpose is served by summarizing the summaries already included in the preceding chapters. I hope I have explored usefully the meaning of responsibility, its status as both goal and requirement in good liberal democracies, its place in our professions, the guidance it can give us, and its justification and limits. Using freedom responsibly is not our fullest end, but it is for each of us a good beginning.

NOTES

1. By arguing in this way I will be countering views that Locke's mature writings (and liberalism) are incoherent in important respects and that we need to find the basis of his unity elsewhere, say in his religious beliefs or political program. Given the purposes of this book, my procedure is to make my case, not to confront opposed scholarly views directly.

2. My view of Locke shares elements with others who believe Locke to be at root coherent. (It also shares elements with those who believe Locke to be essentially incoherent.) How I differ from them will become evident as I proceed, but I will mention several basic points here. For one, I claim that the rational

coherence of Locke's view means to provide an alternative to the security of religious dogma, not merely a complement to belief. This is clearest in Locke's attempt to base his arguments on what is both naturally and commonsensically accessible and secure: simple ideas, and free choice. For another, I claim that the
importance of reason in Locke should not blind us to the limits of his notion of
reason, visible, for example, in the ways that he sees the connections among ideas.
For a third, by claiming that the inner connection among Locke's views of freedom, the self, pleasure, and reason is moral–ontological, I set the question of the
relation between rights and enjoyment on different grounds from where it usually rests. Among the works I have in mind are Richard Ashcraft, *Revolutionary
Politics and Locke's Two Treatises of Government* (Princeton, N.J.: Princeton Univer-
sity Press, 1986); John Dunn, *The Political Thought of John Locke* (Cambridge:
Cambridge University Press, 1969); Ruth W. Grant, *John Locke's Liberalism*
(Chicago: University of Chicago Press, 1987); Peter Laslett, "Introduction" to
Locke's *Two Treatises of Government* (Cambridge: Cambridge University Press,
1988); Peter C. Myers, *Our Only Star and Compass* (Lanham, Md.: Rowman &
Littlefield, 1998); Thomas Pangle, *The Spirit of Modern Republicanism* (Chicago:
University of Chicago Press, 1988); A. John Simmons *The Lockean Theory of
Rights* (Princeton, N.J.: Princeton University Press, 1992); Leo Strauss, *Natural
Right and History* (Chicago: University of Chicago Press, 1953); Nathan Tarcov,
Locke's Education for Liberty (Chicago: University of Chicago Press, 1984); Jeremy
Waldron, *God, Locke and Equality* (Cambridge: Cambridge University Press,
2002); and Michael Zuckert, *Launching Liberalism* (Lawrence: University Press of
Kansas, 2002). Because my task here is primarily theoretical, I will concentrate
mostly on the *Essay Concerning Human Understanding,* published in 1690 with
important changes in the second edition in 1694 and the fourth edition in 1700.
The best contemporary edition, based on the text of the fourth edition, is edited
by Peter Nidditch, Oxford University Press, 1975.

3. *Essay* IV, 16–20.

4. *Essay* III, 10, IV 4.

5. *Essay* IV, 19.

6. *Essay* IV, 15–20.

7. Consider the discussion of tyranny in the *Second Treatise,* chapter 18, and
chapter 4 in this book.

8. *Essay* IV, 10.

9. See also Zuckert's questions about Locke's proof of God's existence, p. 190.

10. For a different conclusion about the importance of Locke's proof of the existence of God to the moral truth of Locke's enterprise see Waldron, pp. 79–80.

11. Consider Pangle, pp. 141–58, 198–209. Indeed, Locke's discussion of assent, faith, and error is conducted in fully secular terms, which he then employs

when he is discussing belief in particular revelation: there is no special capacity of assent engaged by or open to belief strictly (*Essay* IV, 15–20).

12. *Essay* IV, 16. See also his *A Discourse of Miracles*, written in 1702 and published posthumously in 1706. John Locke, *The Reasonableness of Christianity with a Discourse of Miracles and Part of a Third Letter Concerning Toleration,* edited by I. T. Ramsey (Stanford, Calif: Stanford University Press, 1958). (In this edition *Reasonableness* is abridged. For the full text see John Locke, *Works,* volume 7, London, 1823.)

13. Locke himself teaches in the *Second Treatise* that his own "strange doctrine" is in fact a central natural one (*Second Treatise,* II, 9, 13; XVI, 180).

14. See the first chapter of this book and Locke's various Letters on Toleration.

15. *Essay* IV, 17.

16. See also Locke's *Some Thoughts Concerning Education,* number 176. Locke's *Thoughts* were published first in 1693. The best modern edition is edited by John W. and Jean S. Yolton, Oxford University Press, 1989.

17. Reason is not forced to confront belief with sophisticated Socratic arguments, moreover, or with rare and remote natural goods such as full philosophic or political virtue. Rather, the grounds of the natural standpoint available to reason are directly accessible and compelling.

18. Locke's list of primary qualities varies, sometimes not including number, sometimes including bulk and texture.

19. *Essay* II, 11.

20. Locke does not obviously differentiate perception and (self) consciousness but he clearly means to say that when I perceive I always perceive or reflect on an idea as my perception or reflection.

21. *Essay* II, 23. The question of the unity of the will or the self becomes central for many of those who follow Locke. It also becomes a ground to question further the characteristic limits of Locke's view of reason, because seeing connections is central to reason's power. If we look at Hegel or Plato we notice a certain static nature to Locke ideas and the things that cause them in us, and even to what Locke sees as our own constructions. From an Hegelian or Platonic standpoint Locke fails to account for several elements of the essential openness or incompleteness of what appears complete, for how ideas are connected in things and therefore ultimately to each other, and for how we notice this. It would take us too far afield to discuss this issue fully.

22. Locke also discusses modes, at length. Most ideas are modes of simpler ideas. Modes are differences created by variation in the same thing (*Essay* II, 13). The obvious examples are the differences among different numbers. We may therefore find the connections within or among different things in their being variations of more of the same. This does not work very well for the connecting

principle in mixed modes, however, for these are compositions among different ideas.

23. *Essay* II, 26.

24. *Essay* III, 6, 9. Locke eliminates serious consideration of formal and final causes.

25. *Essay* I, 4; II, 1, 14, 18; III, 1.

26. Consider chapters 1 and 7 of this book.

27. *Essay* II, 7, 20

28. See *Thoughts*, numbers 115, 116.

29. Although we could try to differentiate types of uneasiness—pressure, irritation, stiffness, etc.—this would again emphasize what one longs for specifically, and pleasure would lose its simple universal effectiveness.

30. Pleasure covers equally intellectual and bodily pleasure or, strictly for Locke, all pleasures are mental, "different Constitutions of the Mind, sometimes occasioned by disorder in the Body, sometimes by Thoughts of the Mind" (II, 20; II, 7). These notions of pleasure and unease are the basis of the flatness and equality of goods of the self that are correlated to responsibility. Consider the first chapter of this book.

31. *Essay* II, 20, 21. See also *Thoughts*, numbers 107, 116, 128, and the first chapter of this book.

32. Pleasure and what is useful are the goods that are coherent in their meaning and effectiveness with the secure equilibrium of the self. Locke passes by his remarks in the *Essay* about the fit between pleasure, pain, and the use of our senses (too much light hurts our eyes, say) and does not explore the modes of delight because such a path might point away from the identity or equality of pleasure except in amount or accidental source and would not fit simply with the notions of end, composure, and the other correlated ideas I have been discussing. This path also would work against the equality in freedom that grounds Locke's moral, political, and rhetorical purposes.

33. Perhaps we also all can see fairly easily that neither grand nor intense passion nor a mother's love are captured by this notion, let alone raging anger and offended pride.

34. Locke does not invest our full reason and understanding in the very experience of enjoyment—in grasping what is beautiful, in true thought, and so on—but, rather, in accumulating satisfactions and what brings them about. Nonetheless, such complex sources of pleasures at least have their equal place along with the others. The discrimination of liberalism against what is high or complex, the leveling we see even in responsibility, is perhaps the gentlest of such discriminations.

35. *Essay* II, 21.

36. *Essay* II, 21.

37. *Essay* II, 21.

38. *Essay* II, 21.

39. *Essay* II, 21.

40. *Essay* II, 21.

41. *Essay* II, 21.

42. *Essay* II, 7, 21.

43. See *Second Treatise* V, 34, 43; cf. *Essay* II, 21, paragraph 34.

44. On the importance of denying immediate desire and following reason, see also *Thoughts*, numbers 33, 38, 45, 75, 107, and 108. On industry see also *Thoughts*, numbers 94, 123, 126, and 152. Locke does not mention responsibility (as we said, it first is named around the time that *The Federalist* was written.) In *Thoughts* he praises and recommends elements that make it up—for example, in numbers 70, 126, 152, 200, and 201.

45. In addition to the *Two Treatises*, see *Thoughts*, numbers 105–10.

46. Consider Locke's discussion of preservation of self and others in the *Two Treatises*. See also *Thoughts*, numbers 116 and 123–28.

47. *Essay* II, 21, paragraph 34. See *Thoughts*, numbers 33, 38, 46, 52, 75, 94, 119, 129, 122, 126, and 207.

48. In addition to the *Essay* and *Second Treatise* (e.g., V, 34, 48) consider *Thoughts* numbers 33, 36, 52, 73, 81, and 103–105. Consider also Myers, chapter 4.

49. *Second Treatise*: II, 4, 7; V, 16, 25; VIII, 95.

50. As I have pointed out, we can in time develop preferences, or make absences painful, irritating or inconvenient, and we can choose which preferences will determine us in all but the most importunate cases. Not only means but also ends can be chosen, though the most important ends—knowledge, property, justice or fear of punishment—are as much means for others, for "man" generally, as they are ends (and means) for myself.

51. In addition to the *Two Treatises*, see *Thoughts*, number 73. Locke does not name the contemporary virtue of being nice that I discussed in the first chapter. He does, however, make several remarks about other virtues that flow from this root equality, and that are connected to being nice. Consider his remarks on civility, considerateness, kindness, compassion, politeness, good-naturedness, deference, and humanity, not to speak of liberality and justice, in *Thoughts*, numbers 66, 67, 90, 94, 108, 116, 117, 139, and 142–45.

52. Whatever the utility of sociality, moreover, or the status of a natural impulsion to it, it is not for Locke a source of right or political authority: Locke spends much time, for example, telling us why paternal is not political power. Nor does he argue that there is a basic social feeling of sympathy on which to ground politics.

53. For thoughtful arguments that look at this issue (and those of the previous section) and arrive at (somewhat) different conclusions consider, among others, Waldron (who emphasizes as the source of Locke's defense of equality reason's ability to abstract and therefore to know God) and Zuckert (who, emphasizes the priority of our ownership or property in ourselves, although he also remarks the importance of unease.)

INDEX

ABOUT THE AUTHOR

Mark Blitz, A.B and Ph.D. from Harvard University, is Fletcher Jones Professor of Political Philosophy at Claremont McKenna College, where he also has been director of research and chair of the Department of Government. He served during the Reagan administration as associate director of the United States Information Agency, where he was the U.S. government's senior official responsible for educational and cultural exchange, and as senior professional staff member of the Senate Committee on Foreign Relations. He has been vice president and director of political and social studies at the Hudson Institute and has taught political theory at Harvard University and at the University of Pennsylvania. He is the coeditor (with William Kristol) of *Educating the Prince* and the author of *Heidegger's "Being and Time" and the Possibility of Political Philosophy* and of many articles on Greek and German political philosophy, public policy, and foreign affairs.